Edward Taylor
An Annotated Bibliography, 1668--1970

Edward Taylor

An Annotated Bibliography, 1668--1970

By Constance J. Gefvert

University of Minnesota

The Kent State University Press

The Serif Series: Number 19

Bibliographies and Checklists

William White, General Editor
Wayne State University

ISBN 0-87338-113-0
Library of Congress Card Catalog Number 70-144811
Manufactured in the United States of America
at the press of The Oberlin Printing Company
Designed by Merald E. Wrolstad

First Edition

For My Parents

Biographical Note

Although Edward Taylor is now considered the foremost poet of Colonial America, his poetry was virtually unknown until 1937. Much remains obscure about Taylor's early life. He was born in Sketchley, Leicestershire, England, in about 1642. Brought up in a dissenting family and educated in a dissenting school, he remained a staunch Puritan all his life. After the Restoration, his religious convictions made it impossible for him to sign the Act of Uniformity, and so he was not allowed to continue his teaching career. In 1668, after a great deal of harassment for his non-conformist beliefs, Taylor emigrated to Massachusetts Bay. He graduated from Harvard College in 1671, and the same year went to the frontier town of Westfield, Massachusetts, to become pastor of the small Puritan congregation there. He remained in Westfield the rest of his life, acting as both pastor and physician to the townspeople and writing poetry which, unfortunately for his contemporaries, he never published. He retired from his ministry in 1725, exhausted in both body and mind, and died in 1729. His tombstone still stands in the old Westfield cemetery.

Contents

Preface

While the sheer volume of scholarship on Edward Taylor has more than doubled in the last decade, no complete bibliography of Taylor has yet been published. Carol Ann Hoffmann's "Selected Bibliography" (No. 51), published in 1961, was intentionally limited and of course is now much outdated. Mary Jane Elkins' "Checklist" on Edward Taylor (No. 52), published in the Spring 1969 issue of *Early American Literature* and supplemented in later issues, brings Hoffmann's listing of critical articles up to date but is still highly selective.

The purpose of this bibliography, therefore, is to provide a comprehensive list of primary and secondary sources for the study of Edward Taylor. The bibliography aims at completeness in the following sections: *A*, editions of Taylor's works; *B*, letters; *C* and *D*, first publications; *E*, manuscripts; *F*, bibliographies of Taylor alone (no attempt has been made to include bibliographical references to Taylor in literary histories and anthologies or in more comprehensive bibliographies), *H*, books; *J*, articles in periodicals (including reviews); and *K*, doctoral dissertations (the list of other theses in *K* is selective, however). "Completeness" in these sections refers only to publications in English, although as many articles in foreign languages have been included as possible. Section *G*, biography and genealogy, is a complete listing of sources known to date. Section *I*, critical articles in books, is a selective listing. I have not attempted to include every mention of Taylor in anthologies and literary histories; rather, those articles and parts of books which have made significant contributions to Taylor scholarship, or which are important for historical reasons are given.

Title-page transcriptions and descriptions of the physical books are provided for all items in Section A, editions of Taylor's works. In the physical descriptions, only initial and final unnumbered pages are inferred; normally unnumbered internal pages (e.g., divisional title pages and blank pages) are not explicitly noted. The size given is the size of the type page, not the uncut page.

Arrangement of items in Sections *A*, *C*, *D*, and *F* (editions, first publications, and bibliographies) is chronological by date of publication and in Section *B* (letters) chronological by date of composition. Arrangement in Section *E* (manuscripts) is alphabetical first by location of the manuscript, then by title. I have followed the manuscript titles as given by Stanford (No. 3, pp. 502-521), except that the title of No. 36, which was too recently discovered to be included in Stanford's list, is given as in Grabo (No. 188, p. 394).

Items in all other sections are arranged alphabetically by author. In articles of joint authorship, names are listed in the same order as they appear in the article. Within a group of listings by one author, the arrangement is alphabetical first by title (including the interpolated designation [Review]), then by journal, and then by date. Frequent cross-references are given to guide the reader to supplementary or contrasting material. If a page reference is not given, the reader should assume the reference is to the item as a whole.

Throughout the annotations, references to the *Preparatory Meditations* are given with series number, period, and meditation number: *Meditation 2.43* refers to Meditation 43 in the second series. It should be noted that prior to 1960, critics referred to the *Preparatory Meditations* as *Sacramental Meditations*, the title which early scholars erroneously believed was Taylor's, but which Louis Martz discovered was an interpolation by Ezra Stiles (see No. 3, p. vii).

My deepest thanks go to David Smith of Indiana University, who first aroused my interest in Taylor; to Gordon O'Brien of the University of Minnesota, from whom I learned so much about bibliographical investigation; and especially to Edward Griffin of the University of Minnesota, who has encouraged me in this project and generously provided much needed assistance and criticism. I also thank the staff of the Inter-Library Loan Department at the University of Minnesota Libraries, without whose help this project could not have been completed. I am particularly grateful to Florence Gefvert, who typed the manuscript with competence and love, and to Kay Seymour, whose encouragement and patient proofreading have been invaluable.

Minneapolis, Minnesota — Constance J. Gefvert
April 1971

Introduction

In September 1851, more than a century after the death of Edward Taylor, the historian William Sprague wrote a letter to Taylor's great-grandson, Henry Wyllys Taylor, asking him about his ancestor. Sprague was compiling a history of American divinity, which came to be entitled *Annals of the American Pulpit* (1859), and needed information about the Westfield preacher. Henry Taylor obligingly wrote Sprague an answer to his queries; part of his letter, as quoted in the *Annals*, follows:

> Mr. Taylor cannot be said to have possessed a poetic genius of a very high order; but he appears to have had an abiding passion for writing poetry during his whole life. There are extant specimens of his poetical effusions through a period of about sixty-seven years, some of which may justly claim considerable merit. But, previous to his death, he enjoined it upon his heirs never to publish any of his writings. (No. 92, p. 180)

Those "extant specimens" were among the Taylor manuscripts which were kept in the family and which Henry Taylor presented to the Yale University library about thirty years after writing this letter. The letter is interesting for two reasons. First, it is the earliest known comment on Taylor as a poet and indicates that his poetry was not taken very seriously even by those who had seen it. Second, the last sentence has continued to haunt Taylor critics. Did he "enjoin it upon his heirs never to publish" because he feared that his "secret" non-Puritan inclinations would be discovered? Or because of his humility and modesty? Or did he "enjoin" it at all?

A few years later, in 1881, John L. Sibley borrowed information from Sprague's *Annals* when he wrote about Taylor in *Biographical Sketches of Graduates of Harvard University* (No. 85)—the book which most critics of Taylor cite as their authority when they say that Taylor forbade his heirs to publish his poetry. As Francis Murphy has recently established, however, Taylor's supposed injunction against publication is nothing more than family legend, since no record of it exists in the extant writings of Taylor's lifetime and since Taylor left no will (No. 242). Nevertheless, almost all of Taylor's critics since Thomas Johnson have found it necessary to account somehow for his reluctance to publish. As we shall see, this alleged reluctance has been used to support critical estimates of the most varying sorts.

For almost seventy years after Sibley's *Harvard Graduates*, little further comment was made about Taylor as a poet. One of his descendants, John Taylor Terry, privately published a little book about him in 1892 (No. 95). In 1920 Thomas Wright, speaking of the dearth of literature during the colonial years, mentioned that although colonial Americans wrote more poetry than commonly believed, they did not always publish it. "Edward Taylor of Westfield," for instance, "filled a notebook with verse, none of which has ever been published [with one minor exception—see Johnson, No. 212] as the writer forbade publication" (No. 136, p. 162). Even as late as 1939 Josephine Piercy, in a book entitled *Studies of Literary Types*, does not mention Taylor's poetry but discusses his manuscript "Metallographia" in her chapter on "The Scientific Essay" (No. 127, p. 37).

Although all of these writers were aware of the Taylor manuscripts in the Yale library, none took the poems seriously.

Then, in 1935, Thomas H. Johnson made one of the most important literary discoveries of the century (see No. 211). Reading in Sibley's *Harvard Graduates*, he noticed a reference to Taylor's manuscript "Poetical Works" and decided to follow the lead and examine the holdings in the Yale library. Happily he discovered that the manuscripts contained poetry of high quality; Taylor was a genuine poet whose verse had been all but forgotten for over two hundred years. In Johnson's words, "it is questionable, indeed, whether the depth of his poetic imagination and the vigor of his inventive fancy were equaled in verse by any of his countrymen until the nineteenth century. Only the fact that he 'gave orders that his heirs should never publish any of his writings' can account for the obscurity into which his verses were consigned" (No. 1, p. 11).

In 1937, after the long and often difficult task of transcribing the manuscripts, Johnson published several of Taylor's poems and offered a critical evaluation in the *New England Quarterly* (No. 20); two years later he published a substantial selection of the poems as *The Poetical Works of Edward Taylor* (No. 1) —including thirty-one of the *Sacramental Meditations*, five occasional poems, and all of *Gods Determinations*, together with a critical introduction and notes. The history of Taylor scholarship really begins with these publications. It is a history which is important not only for the light it sheds on Taylor, but also for the new insight it has given us into Puritan aesthetic theory and particularly Puritan attitudes toward poetry. Because the later critics are quite different in this respect from the early ones, it will be helpful to discuss the progress of Taylor criticism in terms of three clearly discernible periods.[1]

The earliest phase of Taylor scholarship began in 1937 with

---

[1] Norman Grabo suggests a similar, although not identical, three-fold division in a recent article (No. 191a). I arrived at my grouping independently, having written this introduction before his article was published.

Johnson's *New England Quarterly* article and lasted until the mid-1950s. The period was dominated by a sense of excitement and curiosity over this newly discovered colonial poet so obviously superior to anyone in the accepted canon. For years prior to the discovery, intellectual historians had insisted that the Puritans' attitude toward life denied them the possibility of writing good poetry—anything, that is, more than "versified doctrine." Then suddenly a poet who did not fit that view of Puritanism was discovered: Edward Taylor was ostensibly a Puritan and yet obviously wrote poetry for his own satisfaction rather than for any solely didactic purpose. What seemed even stranger—he wrote poetry that was sensuous and mystical, and he used imagery very much like that of the Anglo-Catholic poets of seventeenth-century England. The problem the critics faced, then, was how to account for this apparent contradiction. Was Taylor only superficially a Puritan with secret leanings toward Catholic mysticism? Most critics, whether they thought Taylor's poetry any good or not, answered affirmatively. For one thing, that theory seemed to explain why he allegedly forbade his heirs to publish his poetry. For another, it reaffirmed their view that Puritanism was not an adequate lifestyle for producing serious poetry.

The other problem preoccupying the early critics was Taylor's poetic ancestry. Whatever tradition they placed him in—metaphysical, baroque, classical—most critics believed that tradition to be in conflict with or restricted by Puritanism. Scholars measured his poetry against the touchstone of that non-Puritan tradition and found him either a success because he could rise above his Puritanism, or a failure because he was unable to transcend his Puritanism to meet the demands of that tradition.

Thomas Johnson, as Taylor's first editor and critic, delineates most of the scholarly problems of the early period—Taylor's literary ancestry, his poetic strengths and weaknesses, the relative value of *Gods Determinations* as against the *Sacramental Meditations*, and the effect of Puritanism on his poetry. One of Johnson's first concerns is to locate Taylor in the tradition of English poetry. Although he does not try to prove direct influence, he demonstrates Taylor's affinity with the metaphysical poets: his "fertility in image-making, tenderness, rapture and delicacy, as well as intense devotion, ally the staunch Puritan with the 'sacred poets' of the early seventeenth century"—especially with Quarles, Herbert, and Crashaw (No. 20, p. 291).

Since Johnson is eager to establish Taylor in this tradition, he concentrates his analysis of Taylor's poetic strengths and weaknesses on a comparison with other metaphysical poets, rather than on a close analysis of his poetic technique *per se.* He asserts, for instance, that Taylor shares with Crashaw "a seraphic exaltation and prodigality of fanciful tropes, passionate outburst, the language of amorous poetry adapted to religious expression, gaudy color, cloying sweetness" (No. 20, p. 319). On the other hand, the quieter aspects of Taylor's verse—his "holy aspiration, his devotion rather than mystical qualities, his homely comparisons, his intimate appeal to the person of Christ" (No. 20, p. 318)—are more reminiscent of Herbert.

More than anything else in the tradition, the conceit is what Johnson feels is most characteristically metaphysical in Taylor's poetry. In fact, he argues that Taylor sometimes had greater poetic control than many of the "sacred poets." At his best he "achieves a striking unity of design by developing one figure. In so doing he avoids a fault to which all sacred poets are commonly prone, that is, strewing metaphors throughout their verses with prodigal abandon" (No. 20, p. 320).

Although Johnson admires this metaphoric unity, he nevertheless feels that Taylor actually achieves it in relatively few of the Meditations. As a sustained work of poetry, he finds the *Sacramental Meditations* uneven in quality. Significantly, in his edition of the *Poetical Works* Johnson prints only thirty-one of the total 221 meditations, for in his opinion their "point of view, the spirit, mood and symbolism is unchanging; only the conceits vary, until the quaint and the unexpected become usual" (No. 20, p. 307). It is *Gods Determinations*, Johnson asserts, which contains Taylor's most successful poetry, for its "inventive fancy," i.e., its great variety of verse forms, makes it less tedious and more interesting than the *Sacramental Meditations* (No. 20, p. 317). Furthermore, its "metaphoric brilliance and unity of design" is more consistent (No. 20, p. 300). Even though Johnson finds greater artistic merit in *Gods Determinations*, he believes that Taylor makes up for technical weaknesses in the *Sacramental Meditations* by the sincerity and expressive power of his devotion. The *Meditations* "are always touching, and indeed they are conceived in a spirit so emotionally intense and sincere that the reader is the more ready to overlook occasional bad rimes or strained figures" (No. 20, p. 317).

Unlike later critics of this period, Johnson finds no conflict between the kind of poetry Taylor wrote and his Puritan theology. Johnson believes that Taylor, like his metaphysical predecessors, was moved to his best poetry by both religious devotion and innate artistic impulse: his "sole inspiration was a glowing, passionate love for Christ, expressed in terms of his own unworthiness and wistful yearning" (No. 1, p. 11). And, in the verses which that inspiration produced, "his vitality as a prosodist and his evident delight in tone and color indicate how thoroughly he enjoyed poetry as an art" (No. 1, p. 11). Johnson assumes that religious devotion and its expression in poetry are as natural in Taylor as in Herbert and Crashaw. Though he expresses surprise and delight at finding a metaphysical style in a Puritan poet, he does not find it at all inconsistent with Taylor's theology.

While subsequent critics in this first period did not of course always agree with Johnson's evaluation of Taylor, they did agree on the importance of the issues Johnson outlined. All attempted to place Taylor in the appropriate tradition, though they did not all agree with Johnson that "metaphysical" was the best description of Taylor's style or that Taylor often surpassed the seventeenth-century poets. They also disagreed widely on the type and seriousness of Taylor's technical deficiencies. And, unlike Johnson, most critics preferred the *Sacramental Meditations* to *Gods Determinations* as Taylor's greatest achievement. Finally, most of these early critics tended either to blame Taylor's deficiencies on the narrowness of the Puritan aesthetic or to assert that Taylor's poetic successes were due to his ability to overcome the limitations of his Puritan beliefs. Interestingly enough, the emphasis on the inconsistency between Taylor the poet and Taylor the Puritan preacher increased between the time of Johnson and Stanford, as each critic, in dialogue with previous scholars, became more and more eager to show that our one good colonial poet was really no Puritan—perhaps because Puritanism was unfashionable and the metaphysical style especially popular at the time they were writing.

Austin Warren, Taylor's first critic after Johnson, thus put less emphasis on the dichotomy between Taylor's poetic practice and theological beliefs than did subsequent scholars. In his 1941 article, "Edward Taylor: Colonial Baroque," Warren agrees with Johnson that Taylor belongs in the tradition of seventeenth-century devotional poets, and for a similar reason. The most characteristic element of his poetry is the homely conceit, the "domesticating" of lofty concepts: "the shock comes from the modernization, the provincializing and localizing of the Infinite, the innocently crude exteriorizations of the Inner" (No. 273, p. 361). Warren, however, prefers "baroque" rather than "metaphysical" as a description of that characteristic use of metaphor. The baroque philosophy, he asserts, is most clearly seen in Roman and Anglo-Catholicism; however "it is not absent from—but only restricted by—Puritanism and Nonconformity: A supernaturalistic treatment of Biblical and apostolic history is common to all seventeenth-century Christians" (No. 273, p. 356). Although Warren states that the baroque style was consistent with Puritanism, in fact he presents Taylor as a kind of anomaly among New England Puritans, thus giving some precedence for later critics to assume that Taylor had "Catholic" or at least non-Puritan tendencies.

Wallace Brown (1944) challenges Warren's use of the term "baroque," asserting that "metaphysical" is a better description of the tight, logical structure which characterizes Taylor's best poems. Interestingly enough, however, the language he uses to describe the metaphysical quality of Taylor's poetry is similar to that which Warren uses to argue that Taylor's poetry is baroque. The difference between them is largely a matter of definition. For instance, Brown shows how Taylor brings together heterogeneous ideas through the "language of sharp contrasts between the abstract erudite and the concrete commonplace . . . the most important effect of these contrasts in metaphysical poetry is the shock or surprise that comes from the domesticating of the Infinite" (No. 159, pp. 189-190).

Because Brown's emphasis is largely on defining "metaphysical" and applying it to Taylor's poetry, he is not especially concerned with whether or not that style is compatible with Taylor's theology and the Puritan aesthetic. Herbert Blau (1953), on the other hand, is concerned more than any previous critic with precisely that problem. He attempts to prove that serious incongruities exist between

Taylor's metaphysical artistry and his Puritanism. For instance, he sees a paradox in Taylor's poetry which is inherent in Calvinistic theology—that is, the apparent contradiction between believing in predestination and ignoring the implications of that doctrine in actual practice. *Gods Determinations*, for instance, belies Calvinistic dogma; there would be no need for repentence if predestination were taken seriously. Blau also maintains that Taylor's rapturous joy at the Lord's Supper is not consistent with a theology in which Christ is not "really present" in that sacrament. Unlike Herbert, whose emotion is understandable because of the Anglican belief in the "Real Presence," for Taylor "there is no excuse. His celebration of the sacraments is motivated by nothing except an intense feeling for the ritual as ritual" (No. 157, p. 338). Blau feels that Taylor is a successful poet only insofar as he transcends those contradictions, and he implies that Taylor could have been a better poet had he avoided them altogether.

William Goodman (1954) is another critic who argues Taylor's affinity with the metaphysical poets. Unlike the others, however, Goodman objects to putting Taylor into a particular literary school. In "Edward Taylor Writes His Love," he demonstrates, by quoting a letter Taylor wrote to Elizabeth Fitch, that it was as "natural" for Taylor to express his devotion to Christ in the language of love as it was for Herbert and Donne (witness the extent to which he used the "Canticles" as texts for his *Sacramental Meditations*). Goodman emphasizes that this metaphoric quality of mind was inherent in Taylor and not merely dependent on a "school" of poetry. What Taylor does in the love letter "is to exhibit the characteristic method of his poetry. . . . The fact for emphasis is that this metaphysical method was thoroughly native to Taylor" (No. 187, p. 514). Consequently, Goodman finds no serious conflict between Taylor's style and his religion.

Other critics of the first phase are concerned with placing Taylor in a literary tradition, but disagree that it is primarily metaphysical or baroque. Nathalia Wright (1946), for example, finds that Taylor's "was a mind more responsive to medieval than to Renaissance influence." She finds this especially true in *Gods Determinations*, where the influence of the medieval morality play is apparent (No. 282, p. 17). Unlike later critics of this period, she is not overly concerned with how that medieval influence squares with Taylor's Puritanism.

Willie Weathers, on the other hand, finds him a "Hellenistic Puritan" (1946), and asserts that Taylor forbade his heirs to publish his verse because he did not want to reveal his secretly unorthodox use of classicism. Intrigued by the vision of a Puritan poet creating a "Calvinistic pantheon" at the expense of orthodox Puritan theology, Weathers tries in a later article (1954) to account for the contradiction by showing Taylor was really a Cambridge Platonist. Possibly anxious to find him an enlightened "universalist" in regard to salvation rather than a dogmatic predestinarian, Weathers seriously misreads *Gods Determinations*, asserting that "everyone," not just the elect, gets saved. With Weathers' criticism, the dichotomy between Taylor's artistry and his avowedly Puritan theology reaches a climax.

Early critics of Taylor, while concentrating most of their attention on the problem of Taylor's literary ancestry and often on the incompatibility between that ancestry and his Puritanism, also examined other issues first suggested by Johnson—especially the relative value of *Gods Determinations* and the *Sacramental Meditations*, and the problem of his poetic strengths and weaknesses.

Nathalia Wright was the only critic to agree with Johnson that *Gods Determinations* is Taylor's most successful poem. Because most critics measured Taylor against the metaphysical touchstone, they tended to prefer the *Meditations*, where they felt the conceit is used most successfully. Nevertheless, although Warren, Brown, and Blau assert that Taylor's best poetry is worthy of the metaphysicals, they agree with Johnson that his work is uneven. Warren asserts that "Taylor is sometimes a neat little artisan, but more often an unsteady enthusiast, a naive original, an intermittently inspired Primitive" (No. 273, p. 37). Blau concurs that Taylor lacked craftsmanship. Whereas Brown had asserted that Taylor at his best truly achieves T. S. Eliot's ideal of the "sensuous apprehension of thought," Blau puts greater emphasis on Taylor's failure to achieve that synthesis. Because his heterogeneous images are sometimes too shocking, they fail to achieve the intended synthesis of finite and infinite. It is a problem which Taylor shares with the other metaphysicals, Blau says, but his "bungling ingenuity and lapses of taste are more palpable than those of the other metaphysical poets, with the possible exception of Crashaw, perhaps because Taylor never refinished his poems for publication" (No. 157, p. 355).

Not all the early critics excused Taylor's technical deficiencies on grounds of his piety, primitivism, or private purpose as Johnson, Warren and Blau did. Sidney Lind (1948) and Roy Harvey Pearce (1950) both find Taylor a mediocre poet at best, and blame his mediocrity largely on his Puritanism. Lind, however, begs the question by assuming that Puritan aesthetic theory was anti-poetic; since Taylor was a Puritan, he therefore must have written bad poetry. Pearce more carefully supports his opinion that Taylor is a mediocre poet, but he too is influenced mainly by his predisposition about Puritan culture. That culture, he says, "cut Taylor down (or should one say, built Taylor up?) to its size. However adequate that culture may have been for major religious experience, it was yet inadequate for major poetry; for it allowed for little play of the individual will—in the last analysis, for little real human drama" (No. 244, p. 43).

Whether or not the Puritan milieu was adequate for producing major poetry was a concern shared by most critics of this first period. Those who evaluated Taylor against the touchstone of the English metaphysical or baroque tradition made the most important contributions to future scholarship, because they examined his poetic technique more closely than did other early critics. None of these early scholars, however, paid sufficiently close attention to Taylor's poetry independent of literary schools.

It is understandable that these critics should have concentrated on placing Taylor in a literary tradition, for they had to compensate for over 200 years of lost time and try to find the appropriate critical niche for this Rip Van Winkle of American literary history. It is likewise understandable that critics of this period—most notably Blau and Weathers—were engrossed with the apparent contradiction between Taylor's poetic practices and Puritan attitudes toward art. After all, two of the most influential scholars of colonial New England (Kenneth Murdock and Perry Miller) had fostered the idea that the Puritans had considered poetry no more than "a little recreation" or "versified doctrine."

The assumption that Taylor's poetry was unorthodox not only perpetrated and reinforced the questionable notion that Puritan theology was inconsistent with a mystical-poetic temperament, but led to some drastic misreadings of Taylor's poems. In the late 1950s and early 1960s, therefore, Taylor's two most energetic editors and critics, Donald E. Stanford and Norman S. Grabo, set out to correct these errors, inaugurating the second phase of Taylor scholarship. The articles written by Stanford, Grabo, and Louis Martz, together with Stanford's edition of Taylor's poems and Grabo's editions of his sermons, deepened the understanding both of Taylor and of Puritanism. Instead of fitting Taylor to the Procrustean bed of their concept of Puritan aesthetics, or assuming he belonged in another tradition, as early critics did, scholars of the late fifties were more objective. They clarified the nature of the Puritan aesthetic, and they established Taylor's orthodoxy once and for all, thereby freeing subsequent critics from preoccupations restraining them from a close analysis of Taylor's poetry on its own merits.

Stanford and Grabo set out deliberately to challenge the opinions of critics like Blau, Weathers, Lind, and Pearce, whose basic presupposition—that orthodox Puritan theology did not admit of a sensuous or purely aesthetic attitude toward poetry—had caused two misconceptions. They had concluded either that Taylor harbored "secret" leanings toward Catholicism and mysticism which were incompatible with Puritanism—namely, in his attitude toward the "Real Presence" of Christ at the Lord's Supper (Blau), and in his "universalism" as manifested in *Gods Determinations* (Weathers)—or that Taylor was a perfectly orthodox Puritan whose religion had consigned him to mediocrity as a poet (Lind and Pearce). In the first place, Stanford and Grabo established that Taylor's mystical attitude toward the Lord's Supper was strictly consistent with Calvinism. In a 1955 article, "Edward Taylor and the Lord's Supper," Stanford shows that Calvin himself "asserted the real spiritual presence of Christ at the Lord's Supper and the union of Christ with the believer" (No. 260, p. 173). Furthermore, he observes, Taylor was not alone among Puritan divines in his mysticism—Cotton Mather too "enjoyed rapturous Communications from Heaven" (No. 260, p. 175).

Grabo reinforces Stanford's position on Taylor's mysticism in his 1959 article, "Catholic Tradition, Puritan Literature, and Edward Taylor." He addresses "the question of Taylor's inherent Catholicism, not to deny it, because it is there, but to suggest that it is thoroughly possible to create a Puritan literature within a Catholic tradition" (No. 189, p. 396). He shows, for instance, that Richard Baxter's "Puritanizing" of the formal meditation influenced many orthodox Puritans (like Cotton Mather and Samuel Willard), and that Taylor could likewise be perfectly orthodox while accepting a mystical-meditational outlook on life. Taylor's reported injunction against publication, whatever its reason, was not the result of his having any "heretical" beliefs to keep secret: "he had no more to hide than had his Boston colleagues . . ." (No. 189, p. 402).

Grabo's editions of Taylor's sermons have significantly contributed to an understanding of the relationship between his life as an orthodox Puritan preacher and his mysticism. In the Introduction to *Christographia* (1962), Grabo demonstrates the close relationship between the sermons and the poems. Since each sermon in the series has a corresponding Meditation based on the same text, Grabo concludes that the Meditation was an outgrowth of the sermon and both together formed one integrated meditational process. Furthermore, in the Introduction to the *Treatise on the Lord's Supper* (1966), Grabo shows that Taylor makes his position on the Lord's Supper very clear, challenging Solomon Stoddard's liberalizing efforts to allow the "unregenerate" to partake of the sacrament. To the end of his life Taylor held the most conservative view in the fight with Stoddard, and had a reputation as a reactionary against attempts to liberalize orthodox Puritanism.

Finally, in his book *Edward Taylor* (1961), Grabo focuses on the integrated quality of Taylor's life. Not only was there no necessary contradiction between Puritan orthodoxy and a mystical attitude toward the sacrament, but there was also no contradiction within Taylor's personality; the active and contemplative aspects of his life were of a piece. "From time to time his writing moved him to think himself soaring above the stars to stand at heaven's door. But that mystical door always opened into the meetinghouse at Westfield, admitting him to the society of Christ to whom he had a special calling in the suburbs of glory in America" (No. 98, p. 173).

While apologists of Taylor's orthodoxy gave most attention to his mystical attitude toward the Lord's Supper and its poetic expression, they also addressed two other misunderstandings perpetrated by earlier critics. One such misunderstanding was the belief that Taylor was a universalist in regard to salvation, a view most strongly upheld by Willie Weathers. In a 1960 article on Taylor's sermons, Stanford notes that the following passage from Sermon 10 of *Christographia* should still any doubts about Taylor as a rigidly orthodox predestinarian:

> All the Whole Bundle of the Shining Beams of Executive Love in the Godhead, streame forth through Christ upon the Church onely. This sun shines onely upon that plot. . . . God so Loved the World i.e. the Elect World and not the World opposed to the Elect. (No. 132, p. 10)

With that evidence from Taylor's own pen, it is practically impossible to believe that in *Gods Determinations Touching his Elect*, "elect" refers to "everyone."

In the same article, Stanford challenges the other misunderstanding—that Puritanism was inadequate for producing major poetry. Taylor's weaknesses were no more caused by enslavement to his theology than his successes were due to an ability to transcend that theology. On the contrary, Stanford argues, "it was his rigid Calvinism which motivated his most powerful writing in poetry and prose. For he was convinced he was of the Elect, and for the Elect, double predestination has no terror, but rather an overwhelming conviction of the mercy, the sweetness, and the glory of God" (No. 132, p. 10).

The second period of Taylor scholarship culminated in the

1960 appearance of *The Poems of Edward Taylor*, edited by Stanford and with an important Foreword by Louis Martz. This edition served to establish, for the most part, answers to the various problems and questions regarding Taylor's orthodoxy which had been current since at least the time of Blau. Where Johnson had printed only a selection of the *Meditations*, Stanford published all 217, thereby shifting emphasis from *Gods Determinations* to the meditational aspect of his poetic career. Also Stanford's glossary of terms is considerably different from the glossary Johnson provided in his edition of Taylor's *Poetical Works*. Johnson's glossary had misled some critics into believing Taylor a "universalist" in regard to the idea of election—that is, one who believes that Grace is available to all who will accept it. Stanford's glossary draws directly on definitions from Taylor's own sermons and other writings, unquestionably establishing Taylor as a strict predestinarian. Finally, Stanford's Introduction to *The Poems* summarizes and re-emphasizes his estimate of Taylor as a "mystical" poet whose mysticism was fully consistent with orthodox Calvinist theology.

Part of the impact of Stanford's edition was due to Louis Martz's Foreword. Not only did Martz help to reinforce the image of Taylor as an orthodox Puritan and treat the mystical aspects of Taylor's verse more fully, but he prefigured some of the important concerns of critics to follow in the 1960s. In the first place, Martz emphasizes that "meditative" is a more descriptive and less confining term than "metaphysical" or "baroque." By showing that "meditative" describes a purpose and sometimes a structure but not a specific style, Martz opened the way for an examination of structure and language in Taylor's poetry not bound by preconceived notions of what the metaphysical conceit or baroque sensuousness should be like. The poetic meditation, as Martz demonstrates, is "a verbal action developed through every resource that language can offer" (No. 114, p. xxxiv). Later critics of the third phase are in fact more sensitive to those various resources of the language Taylor used and less inclined to look for certain preconceived kinds of imagery.

Martz also acknowledges some strength in *Gods Determinations* but feels it is not Taylor's greatest achievement; it remains "a labor of versified doctrine . . . in the end, Taylor's standing as a poet must be measured by a full and careful reading of the *Meditations*" (No. 114, p. xiii). And indeed most critical energy of the sixties has been expended on the *Meditations*. Finally, Martz evaluates the extent to which Taylor's Americanism both strengthened and hindered his poetic technique—his language, his homely metaphors, his syntax, and prosody. The peculiarly non-artistic environment of colonial America (not anti-artistic, as intellectual historians previously argued) accounts for Taylor's technical deficiencies. But Martz also recognizes that Taylor's metrical roughness, and other individual characteristics of his poems, sometimes increase the strength of his verse. "Out of his very deficiencies he creates a work of rugged and original integrity. The result helps to mark the beginning of an American language, an American literature" (No. 114, pp. xxxvi-xxxvii).

The criticism of Stanford, Martz, and Grabo laid to rest the problem of the Puritan poet as an apparent anomaly and established Taylor's orthodoxy. Critics of the 1960s, more concerned with Taylor as craftsman, could no longer dismiss his poetic deficiencies either by simply blaming them on his Puritanism or by declaring that his sincerity, primitivism, or fervent devotion compensate for them. In this third period of Taylor scholarship, critics have had to ask new questions, and have had to formulate answers from a closer analysis of the poems. Where does Taylor's poetry succeed and where does it fail? To what extent did Taylor consciously control his imagery? Was he a "primitive" as Johnson and some of the early critics thought him, or did he work at his poems as a conscious craftsman? How skillfully do language, imagery, prosody and structure reinforce his poetic themes? What place does Taylor occupy in the American literary tradition?

One of the most prevalent of these questions is the problem of Taylor as a primitive. Donald Junkins (1965), for instance, argues that Taylor was a conscious artist and sets out to correct the misunderstanding "that Taylor is a powerful poet yet unskilled, and for the specific reason that he is negligent as a craftsman" (No. 219, p. 135). He uses some revisions of the *Meditations* that were found stuffed in the binding of the "Poetical Works" manuscript as proof that Taylor was striving for particular effects. He also substantiates Grabo's opinion that Taylor's roughness was often deliberate: "The revisions show that Taylor was indeed conscious of technique and worked hard to achieve different effects, that he had a good ear for rhythm and clear detail, and that he was able to create the specific poetic effect he wished by achieving smoother lines, sharper images, simpler syntax, and more dramatic expression" (No. 219, p. 136).

Peter Thorpe (1966) supports Junkins by arguing that the irregularities in Taylor's poetic technique are often functional. For instance, the seemingly "inconsistent" imagery is purposeful, for "Taylor without certainty is groping his way towards the light. . . . I can imagine no better way to suggest this middle feeling of uncertainty than through the use of inconsistent imagery" (No. 269, p. 369). Sometimes Thorpe seems to be straining too hard to explain away all the irregularities of Taylor's verse, and some critics would accuse him of what Yvor Winters has called the "fallacy of imitative form." But at least he is evaluating Taylor by aesthetic, instead of merely ideological or historical criteria.

Other critics develop aspects of Junkins' and Thorpe's arguments in greater detail. William Manierre (1962) and Kenneth Ball (1970), for instance, both analyze Taylor's use of traditional rhetoric. Manierre discusses the structural function of Taylor's verbal wit and observes that devices like ploce and polyptoton are "as much a part of Taylor's method as are such oft-discussed characteristics as far-fetched metaphors, puns, homely images and peculiarities of diction . . ." (No. 229, p. 296). Ball (No. 152) considers the way Taylor uses the traditional figures of amplification and meiosis to reinforce themes of God's glory and man's unworthiness. Much critical attention is also directed at the sources of Taylor's images and the way he modified them for his purposes. Several critics, for example, study his use of the "tree of life" image (Brumm, No. 160; Halbert, No. 202; Hedberg, No. 203; and Werge, No. 278), while others analyze his use of typology (Brumm, No. 104; Clendenning, No. 169; Davis, No. 177; Keller, No. 224; and Reiter, No. 249).

The relationship of theme and structure is another area which has received much attention from contemporary critics. E. F. Carlisle (1968), for instance, applies R. F. Blackmur's categories of "evident form" and "deep form" to Taylor's *Meditations* in order to evaluate the way his poetry is structured by the tensions inherent in a Puritan view of life. Carlisle asserts that while the contrast between the "deep form" (often, in Taylor, a meditative structure) is less sharp than in other poets because Taylor's conscious and unconscious view of the world was more unified, nevertheless a distinction between the two can provide a meaningful way of comparing and evaluating individual poems (No. 165). Other critics concerned with structure are Bach (No. 150), Garrison (No. 184), Griffith (No. 200), and Lang (No. 225).

Finally, where the earliest critics were especially concerned with Taylor's literary ancestry, more recent critics have been concerned with his spiritual descendents. Jared Curtis, for example, compares him to Emily Dickinson (No. 174); Michael Colacurcio (No. 173) sees in *Gods Determinations* a profound sense of audience not equalled again until Franklin; and Karl Keller (Nos. 222, 224) deals with the typically American character of Taylor's meditations and with Taylor as a "version" of Emerson.

This recent emphasis on Taylor's Americanism has brought us a long way from the earliest attempts to place him in the English metaphysical tradition. The discovery of Taylor's poetry coincided with the metaphysical revival of the 1930s and 1940s—no wonder, then, that early critics were enthusiastic. Not only was Taylor's achievement far greater than that of any poet in the hitherto accepted canon of colonial literature, but he also was happily "metaphysical" in a time when critics were enthusiastic over the revival of interest in Donne and other English metaphysical poets. As with the history of twentieth-century criticism in general, however, a fuller understanding of Taylor was possible only when critics could escape the predispositions of a certain style and evaluate the poems in a wider context—the entire American literary tradition, which of course includes far more than its English inheritance.

Criticism of Taylor's poetry has, in fact, done a great deal more than merely increase our understanding of Taylor. It has forced us to reappraise our entire conception of Puritan aesthetic theory and hence also of early American intellectual history. As Norman Grabo has suggested, an understanding of a people's attitude toward poetry can come only from observing their actual poetic practice, and not merely from reading what they say about their practice; for example, "terms proper to mysticism are far more abundant [in Puritan literature] than we ordinarily suppose—abundant enough to warrant calling them common" (No. 197, p. 508). Where Cotton Mather formerly seemed unusual in his "reeling and staggering," because our view of Puritanism was too narrow to account for it, recent criticism of Taylor has forced us to reappraise that view. Instead of considering both Mather and Taylor anomalies, it seems more objective and honest to see if our view of the tradition should not be broadened to account for the "mysticism" they share with other Puritans. And this is precisely the benefit of Taylor scholarship. As Grabo has insisted, accepting Taylor's mysticism as a part of the Puritan tradition adds a new dimension to American intellectual history for which scholars like Perry Miller have previously been unable to account "and which might need no accounting were it not for its pervasiveness in the New England temperament, part of the shape of human feeling in the seventeenth century. That is what Taylor's poetry makes so clear" (No. 197, p. 509). In short, the discovery of Edward Taylor's poetry has not only provided us with a new corpus of American poetry, but has had a profound effect on our understanding of American Puritanism and our way of looking at American intellectual history.

I. Primary Sources

A. Editions of Poems and Sermons

(Chronologically arranged)

1 THE / POETICAL / WORKS / OF / EDWARD / TAYLOR / *Edited with an Introduction and Notes by* / THOMAS H. JOHNSON / [rule] / ROCKLAND EDITIONS • NEW YORK. [1939]

Colophon: [ornament] / 925 COPIES OF THIS EDITION / HAVE BEEN PRINTED FOR ROCKLAND EDITIONS / AT THE SPIRAL PRESS • NEW YORK / SEPTEMBER • 1939.

Collation: (7 5/16 x 4 5/16) $[1\text{-}15]^8$, 120 leaves (first and last leaf glued to inside covers); pp. [4] [1-8] 9-231 [232] [4].

Contents: [1] half title: THE POETICAL WORKS OF / EDWARD TAYLOR; [2] blank; [3] title page as above; [4] notice of copyright, printing; [5-7] CONTENTS; [8] blank; 9-10 FOREWORD, signed T. H. J. / 5 February 1939 / Lawrenceville, New Jersey; 11-28 [Introduction]; [29] divisional title page: *Gods Determinations Touching His Elect*: / AND / *The Elects Combat In Their Conversion*, / AND / *Coming Up to God In Christ*: / TOGETHER WITH / *The Comfortable Effects Thereof*; [30] blank; 31-109 text; [110] blank; [111] div.t.p.: FIVE POEMS; [112] blank; 113-119 text; [120] blank; [121] div.t.p.: SACRAMENTAL MEDITATIONS; [122] blank; 123-179 text; [180] blank; 181-187 GLOSSARY; [188] blank (with correction slip pasted on); 189-199 NOTES TO THIS EDITION; [200] blank; 201-220 TAYLOR'S LIBRARY; 221-228 A DESCRIPTION OF THE MANUSCRIPT "POETICAL WORKS"; 229-231 BIBLIOGRAPHY; [232] colophon as above.

The first edition of Taylor's poems in book form. Contains 31 of the Meditations, all of *Gods Determinations*, and miscellaneous poems. The introduction to Taylor and his poetry is an important early essay establishing Taylor in the English metaphysical tradition. The glossary, though challenged by Stanford in regards to certain theological points, is still useful. The listing of books in Taylor's library is invaluable, but the bibliography is now outdated.

Reviewed in Nos. 137, 146, 156, 176, 185, 207, 215, 270, and 279.

2 THE / POETICAL / WORKS / OF / EDWARD / TAYLOR / *Edited with an Introduction and Notes by* / THOMAS H. JOHNSON / [rule] / PRINCETON UNIVERSITY PRESS • PRINCETON. [1943]

Colophon, Collation, and Contents exactly the same as No. 1.

3 THE POEMS OF / [within a dotted rule] Edward Taylor / EDITED BY / Donald E. Stanford / *Associate Professor of English* / *Louisiana State University* / WITH A FOREWORD BY / Louis L. Martz / *Professor of English* / *Yale University* / NEW HAVEN / Yale University Press. [1960]

Collation: (6 15/16 x 3 9/16) [1-19]^{16}, 304 leaves; pp. [2] [i-vi] vii-lxii, 1-543 [544].

Contents: [2] blank; [i] half title: THE POEMS OF EDWARD TAYLOR; [ii] blank; [iii] title page as above; [iv] notice of copyright, printing, reservation of rights; [v] dedication: FOR YVOR WINTERS / *Among the first and farthest*; [vi] blank; vii-viii Preface, signed D. E. S. / *Baton Rouge* / *January 1959*; ix Contents; [x] blank; xi-xii Abbreviations; xiii-xxxvii Foreword BY LOUIS L. MARTZ; [xxxviii] blank; xxxix-lxii Introduction BY DONALD E. STANFORD; 1 *Prologue*; [2] blank; [3] divisional title page: Preparatory Meditations before my / Approach to the Lords Supper. Chiefly / upon the Doctrin preached upon / the Day of administration; 5-80 text of first series; [81] div.t.p.: Preparatory Meditations / SECOND

SERIES; [82] blank; 83-384 text of second series; [385] div.t.p.: Gods Determinations touch- / ing his Elect: and / The Elects Combat in their / Conversion, and / Coming up to God in Christ / together with the / Comfortable Effects thereof.; [386] blank; 387-459 text; [460] blank; [461] div.t.p.: Miscellaneous Poems; [462] blank; 463-498 text; 499-501 Appendix 1. Editions; 502-521 Appendix 2. Manuscripts; [522] blank; 523-543 Glossary; [544] blank.

Plate: facsimile page from the manuscript "Poetical Works" facing p. [iii] (recto blank).

Based on Stanford's doctoral dissertation (No. 304). The most complete edition of Taylor's poems. Inclusion of all the *Preparatory Meditations* as well as *Gods Determinations* and miscellaneous poems reflects Stanford's opinion that the *Meditations* are Taylor's best work.

Includes a Foreword by Louis Martz (No. 114), placing Taylor in the tradition of meditative poets; an Introduction by the editor; a Glossary which differs from Johnson's on some important theological points; and the most complete description of the Taylor manuscripts.

Reviewed in Nos. 198, 147, 162, 171, 175, 179, 182, 195, 201, 204, 206, 210, 217, 230, 232, 238, 253, 257, 266, 271, 274, and 277.

4 EDWARD TAYLOR'S / *CHRISTOGRAPHIA* / EDITED BY NORMAN S. GRABO / [broken rule] / New Haven and London, Yale University Press, 1962.

Collation: (7 1/4 x 4 5/16) $[1\text{-}16]^{16}$ $[17]^{8}$ $[18]^{16}$, 280 leaves; pp. [2] [i-x] xi-xlviii, [1-2] 3-507 [508-510].

Contents: [i] half title: EDWARD TAYLOR'S *CHRISTOGRAPHIA*; [ii] blank; [iii] title page as above; [iv] notice of copyright, printing, reservation of rights, publication grant; [v] dedication: TO PHILIP C. DURHAM; [vi] blank; [vii] Acknowledgments, signed N. S. G. / *East Lansing, Michigan / September 1961*; [viii] blank; [ix] Contents; [x] blank; xi-xliv Introduction; xlv-xlviii A Note on the Text; [1] full title: CHRISTOGRAPHIA. / or / A Discourse to[u]ching Christs Person, / Natures, the Personall Union of the / Natures,

Qualifications, and Oper- / ations Opened, Confirmed, and Practi- / cally improoved in Severall Sermons / delivered upon Certain Sacrament Dayes / unto the Church and people of God in / *Westfield*; [2] blank; 3-468 text; 469-475 Appendix: Taylor's Marginal Notes; 476-493 Explanatory Notes; [494] blank; 495-507 Index; [508-510] blank.

Plate: facsimile page of "Christographia" manuscript facing p. 452 (verso blank).

Based on Grabo's doctoral dissertation (No. 291). Contains 14 sermons on the nature of Christ, preached on sacrament days from August 1701 to October 1703. Includes an important Introduction which discusses the relationship between the sermons and their corresponding *Preparatory Meditations* (Meditations 2.42-56), especially in relationship to Taylor's method of composition.

Reviewed in Nos. 148, 168, 227, 258, 259, and 264.

5 A TRANSCRIPT / OF / EDWARD TAYLOR'S / METRICAL HISTORY OF CHRISTIANITY / by / Donald E. Stanford / Professor of English / Louisiana State University / Baton Rouge, Louisiana. [1962]

Colophon: Reproduced by DUOPAGE process / in the United States of America / MICRO PHOTO INC. / Cleveland 12, Ohio.

Collation: [5 3/8 x 6 3/4] 221 leaves; pp. [2] i-iii [iv], 1-434 [435-436].

Contents: [leaf 1 recto] title page as above; [verso] notice of copyright; i-iii PREFACE, signed D. E. S. / Durham, North Carolina / April, 1962; [iv] blank; 1-434 text; [435] blank; [436] colophon as above.

First publication of the untitled manuscript poem attributed to Taylor (No. 39).

6 THE POEMS OF / [within dotted rule] Edward Taylor / EDITED BY / Donald E. Stanford / NEW HAVEN AND LONDON / Yale University Press. [1963]

Collation: (6 11/16 x 4) [paperbound], 208 leaves; pp. [i-vi] vii-xxxv [xxxvi], 1-369 [370-380].

Contents: [i] half title: THE POEMS OF EDWARD TAYLOR; [ii] plate (see below); [iii] title page as above; [iv] notice of copyright, printing, reservation of rights; [v] dedication: FOR YVOR WINTERS / *Among the first and farthest*; [vi] blank; vii Contents; [viii] blank; ix-x Abbreviations; xi-xxxv Introduction, signed DONALD E. STANFORD / *Baton Rouge, Louisiana / January 1963*; [xxxvi] blank; 1 *Prologue*; [2] blank; [3] divisional title page: Preparatory Meditations before my / Approach to the Lords Supper. Chiefly / upon the Doctrin preached upon / the Day of administration; [4] blank; 5-80 text; [81] div.t.p.: Preparatory Meditations / SECOND SERIES; [82] blank; 83-259 text; [260] blank; [261] div.t.p.: Gods Determinations touch- / ing his Elect; and / The Elects Combat in their / Conversion, and / Coming up to God in Christ / together with the / Comfortable Effects thereof.; [262] blank; 263-335 text; [336] blank; [337] div.t.p.: Miscellaneous Poems; [338] blank; 339-347 text; [348] blank; 349-369 Glossary; [370] blank; [371-374] publisher's list of Yale paperbounds; [375-380] blank.

Plate: facsimile page of "Poetical Works" manuscript on p. [ii].

The second, abridged edition of No. 3. Includes a substantial number of the *Preparatory Meditations*, miscellaneous poems, and all of *Gods Determinations*; and a new Introduction by the editor.

7 [within double rules] The Diary of Edward Taylor / *Edited with an Introduction by* / FRANCIS MURPHY / [drawing of ship enclosed in circle] / Connecticut Valley Historical Museum / Springfield, Massachusetts • • 1964.

Collation: (8 1/4 x 5) [1-5]^4, 20 leaves; pp. [1-6] 7-40.

Contents: [1] half-title: The Diary of Edward Taylor; [2] blank; [3] title page as above; [4] CREDITS [within a double rule], notice of copyright, printing; [5] *Preface*, signed JULIETTE TOMLINSON / *Director* [The Connecticut Valley Historical Museum]—November 1964; [6] ACKNOWLEDGMENTS [within a double rule]; 7-22 *Introduction*; [23] full title: The Diary of Edward Taylor: / AN ATLANTIC VOYAGE /

LIFE AT HARVARD COLLEGE AND / SETTLEMENT AT WESTFIELD, 1668-1672; [24] blank; 25-40 text.

First published in No. 33. The introduction and bibliographical footnotes have been added in this edition.

8 *Edward Taylor's Treatise / Concerning the Lord's Supper /* [ornament] / Edited by / NORMAN S. GRABO / *Michigan State University Press* / 1966.

Collation: (7 1/4 x 3 11/16) [1-10]^{16}, 160 leaves; pp. [i-viii] ix-lvi, 1-263 [264].

Contents: [i] half-title: *Edward Taylor's Treatise / Concerning the Lord's Supper*; [ii] blank; [iii] title page as above; [iv] dedication: For Leon Howard, notice of copyright, printing, printer's device; [v] *Acknowledgments*; [vi] blank; [vii] *Contents*; [viii] blank; ix-xlvii *Introduction*; xlviii-li *Footnotes to the Introduction*; [lii] blank; liii-lvi *A Note on the Text*; 1-221 text; [222] blank; 223-244 *Explanatory Notes*; 245-254 *Index of Biblical References*; 255-263 *General Index*; [264] blank.

A modernized annotated text of 8 sermons preached in 1693 and 1694 against the liberal Stoddardean view of the Lord's Supper. Introduction contains a thorough discussion of the issues involved in Stoddard's controversy with the Mathers and Taylor over the Lord's Supper as a "converting ordinance."

Reviewed in Nos. 145, 170, 240, 243, and 265.

9 THE / POETICAL / WORKS / OF / EDWARD / TAYLOR / *Edited with an Introduction and Notes by* / THOMAS H. JOHNSON / [rule] / PRINCETON UNIVERSITY PRESS. [1966]

Collation: (6 1/2 x 4 7/8) [paperbound], 112 leaves; pp. [1-8] 9-231 [232].

Contents: Same as in No. 1, except: [8] FOREWORD TO THE PAPERBACK EDITION, signed T. H. J. / 10 November 1965 / Lawrenceville, New Jersey; [231] brief BIBLIOGRAPHICAL POSTSCRIPT at bottom of page; [232] colophon missing.

With the minor exceptions noted, this volume is a reprinting of the original 1939 Spiral Press edition (No. 1). It's chief value is historical, in making available in paperback the earliest edition of Taylor's poems. It had already been superseded (1960) by Stanford's much more complete collection of Taylor's poetry (No. 3.)

Reviewed in Nos. 142 and 194.

B. Letters

(Chronologically arranged by date of composition)

10 [Letter to Elizabeth Fitch, Westfield, September 8, 1674.] In Goodman, No. 187, pp. 512-514.

Newly transcribed from a photostat of the manuscript "Poetical Works." Previously printed, but with some inaccuracies, in Caulkins, No. 56, p. 155; Lockwood, No. 72, pp. 40-42 and No. 73, I, 156-158; Terry, No. 94, pp. 132-133 and No. 95, pp. 16-19; and Westfield Jubilee, No. 97, pp. 157-159.

11 [Letter to the Council at Hartford, 1676.] Excerpts in Lockwood, No. 73, I, 237-238.

Concerns the decision to remain in Westfield during King Philip's War. Attributed to Taylor by Lockwood.

12 [Letter to the Council at Hartford, March 15, 1676.] In Lockwood, No. 73, I, 226-228.

A request for reimbursement for quartering Hartford soldiers during King Philip's War. Attributed to Taylor by Lockwood.

13 [Letter to the Council at Boston, April 3, 1676.] In *Westfield Jubilee*, No. 97, pp. 125-126.

Excerpts in Sibley, No. 85, pp. 403-404. Reprinted in Lockwood, No. 73, I, 234-236. Describes the decision of the citizens of Westfield to remain there during King Philip's War. Attributed to Taylor by Lockwood and Bates (see No. 97, p. 59).

14 [Letter to the Massachusetts General Court, May 15, 1679.] In Lockwood, No. 73, I, 189-191.

A letter concerning a land controversy. Signed only with initials, and attributed by Lockwood to Edward Taylor and Thomas Noble.

15 [Letter to the churches of Norwich, Windsor, Springfield, Northampton, and Hadley, July, 1679.] In Lockwood, No. 72, pp. 37-38.

Reprinted in Lockwood, No. 73, I, 109-110. Invites representatives of neighboring churches (including Taylor's father-in-law, James Fitch of Norwich) to attend the formal organization of the Westfield church.

16 [Letter from] "Edward Taylor to Increase Mather," [March 22, 1682/3]. In *The Mather Papers. Massachusetts Historical Society Collections*, Fourth Series, VIII (1868), 629-631.

Describes a hailstorm of July 26, 1682, a strange light in the sky on August 16, 1681, and other strange phenomena.

17 [Letter to Samuel Sewall, Westfield, August 14, 1686.] Extract printed after last page in Cotton Mather. *Right Thoughts in Sad Hours*. London: Thomas Astwood, Printer, 1689, p. [55].

A condolence letter to Sewall including stanzas 5 and 7 of "Upon Wedlock and Death of Children" and apparently given by Sewall to the printer without Taylor's knowledge. Reprinted in Johnson, No. 212, p. 140.

18 "A Letter sent to the Reverend Mr. Solomon Stoddard . . ." [February 13, 1687/8]. In Grabo, No. 192, pp. 198-200.

Transcribed from the manuscript "Commonplace Book" in the Massachusetts Historical Society. Attacks Stoddard's liberalizing innovations in allowing the "unregenerate" to partake of the Lord's Supper.

C. First Publication of Poems in Works Not by Taylor

(Chronologically arranged)

19 [Stanzas 5 and 7 of] "Upon Wedlock and Death of Children." In Cotton Mather. *Right Thoughts in Sad Hours.* London: Thomas Astwood, Printer, 1689, p. [56].

The only publication of any of Taylor's verses during his lifetime. Taylor had included the verses in a condolence letter to Samuel Sewall on the death of one of Sewall's children (see No. 17), and apparently without Taylor's knowledge Sewall sent the letter with verses to Mather, who published it at the end of *Right Thoughts*. Verses reprinted in Johnson, No. 1, pp. 117-119; No. 20, pp. 292-293; No. 212, p. 139; and Stanford, No. 3, p. 468.

20 Johnson, Thomas H. "Edward Taylor: A Puritan 'Sacred Poet.'" *New England Quarterly*, x (1937), 290-322.

First publication (except No. 19) of any of Taylor's poetry. Includes "Huswifery"; "Upon Wedlock and Death of Children"; "The Ebb and Flow"; excerpts from *Gods Determinations*; *Sacramental Meditations* 1.1, 7, 8, 25, 38, "The Experience," "The Reflexion," 2.3, and 112; "Prologue"; and eight lines from "My Last Declamation in the Colledge Hall"—all from the manuscript "Poetical Works." All except the last are reprinted in Johnson, No. 1, pp. 123-179, *passim*; and Stanford, No. 3, pp. 1-287, *passim*. The last is reprinted in Johnson, No. 23, pp. 518-526.

Important first critical study. Delineates most of the issues dealt with in subsequent Taylor criticism. Identifies Taylor with the English tradition and establishes his worthiness to be compared with it. Feels Taylor the Puritan is an anomaly because his poetry is in the Anglican-Roman Catholic tradition. Does not blame Taylor's poetic weaknesses on his Puritanism; rather, considers him something of a primitive whose sincerity and enthusiasm make up for lack of technical polish. Prefers *Gods Determinations* to the *Sacramental Meditations* because they display a greater variety of verse forms. Many of the *Meditations* he includes use extended conceits, the ones he considers the most characteristically metaphysical.

21 "Address to the Soul Occasioned by a rain [*sic*]." *Saturday Review of Literature*, September 2, 1939, p. 8.

First publication of this poem from the manuscript "Poetical Works." Reprinted in Johnson, No. 1, p. 113; and in Stanford, No. 3, p. 463 under title "[When] Let by rain."

22 Johnson, Thomas H. "Some Edward Taylor Gleanings." *New England Quarterly*, XVI (1943), 280-296.

First publication of the following poems from the manuscript "Poetical Works": "Upon a Wasp Chilled with Cold," "Huswifery II," "Upon the Sweeping Flood," and Meditations 1.3, 10, 27, 40, 47, 2.40, 80, and 114. All reprinted in Stanford, No. 3, pp. 7-90, 465-471, *passim.*

Johnson feels that although *Gods Determinations* is Taylor's best work, a few of the Meditations not previously published by him in Nos. 1 or 20 merit publication. Hence, "a final culling is here undertaken lest any of the significant unpublished verses have been inadvertantly neglected."

23 ———. "The Topical Verses of Edward Taylor." *Colonial Society of Massachusetts Publications*, XXXIV (1943), 513-554.

First publication (except for the first 8 lines of the "Declamation"—see Johnson, No. 20) of the following poems from the first 35 pages of the manuscript "Poetical Works": "My Last Declamation in the Colledge Hall May 5, 1671"; two love poems to Elizabeth Fitch; elegies on Zechariah Symmes, Francis Willoughby, John Allen, Charles Chauncy,

Elizabeth Fitch Taylor, Samuel Hooker, Mehetabel Woodbridge, and Increase Mather; and finally the satirical "Verses made upon Pope Joan." The elegies on Samuel Hooker and on Taylor's wife are reprinted in Stanford, No. 3, pp. 471-485.

Johnson considers these topical verses all of social-historical-biographical importance rather than of literary value. The acrostic poems especially are "more admirable for their ingenuity than for succinctness or power."

24 Neufeld, Morris A. "A Meditation Upon the Glory of God." *Yale University Library Gazette*, XXV (1951), 110-111.

First publication of Meditation 1.21. Reprinted in Stanford, No. 3, pp. 35-36.

25 Simison, Barbara D. "Poems by Edward Taylor," *Yale University Library Gazette*, XXVIII (1954), 93-102.

First publication of Meditations 1.2, 13, 22, 24, 26, 32 and 34. All reprinted in Stanford, No. 3, pp. 5-55, *passim*.

26 ———. "Poems by Edward Taylor." *Yale University Library Gazette*, XXVIII (1954), 161-170

First publication of Meditations 1.35, 39, 43, 46, and 2.4. All reprinted in Stanford, No. 3, pp. 56-88, *passim*.

27 ———. "Poems by Edward Taylor." *Yale University Library Gazette*, XXIX (1954), 25-34.

First publication of Meditations 2.19, 25, 29, 37, 41, and 42. All reprinted in Stanford, No. 3, pp. 113-159, *passim*.

28 ———. "Poems by Edward Taylor." *Yale University Library Gazette*, XXIX (1954), 71-80.

First publication of Meditations 2.43, 46, 49, 64, 65, 69. All reprinted in Stanford, No. 3, pp. 159-209, *passim*.

29 Stanford, Donald E. "*Sacramental Meditations* by Edward Taylor." *Yale University Library Gazette*, XXXI (1956), 61-75.

First publication of the following Meditations, which relate to Taylor's controversy with Stoddard over the Lord's

Supper, and which demonstrate Taylor's orthodoxy: 2.104, 105, 106, 107, 108, 109, 111. All reprinted in Stanford, No. 3, pp. 269-282, 284-286.

30 ———. "Nineteen Unpublished Poems by Edward Taylor." *American Literature*, XXIX (1957), 18-46.

First publication of the following Meditations: 1.16, 18, 23, 31, 36, 41, 45, 48; 2.8, 16, 17, 26, 27, 28, 75, 78, 79, 84, 95. All reprinted in Stanford, No. 3, pp. 28-253, *passim*.

Earlier editorial selectivity has made Taylor seem like a "modified Anglican or a neo-Platonist rather than the Calvinist he actually was." These poems help to balance the picture and demonstrate the shifts of mood throughout the Meditations from "extreme spiritual depression" to "equally extreme spiritual exaltation."

31 ———. "The Giant Bones of Claverack, New York, 1705." *New York History*, XL (1959), 47-61.

First publication of "The Giant Bones of Claverack" from the manuscript "Poetical Works."

32 ———. "The Earliest Poems of Edward Taylor." *American Literature*, XXXII (1960), 136-151.

First publication of some poems written before 1669, contained in the manuscript "Diary, Theological Notes, and Poems." Included are "The Lay-mans Lamentation . . . ," a satire on the Act of Uniformity; "A Letter sent to his Brother Joseph Taylor and his wife after a visit" (an acrostic poem); ["A Dialogue between the writer and a Maypole Dresser"]; a poem "in a Letter I sent to my schoolfellow. W. M."; and "An other answer . . . ," an answer to a Popish poem, in a kind of dialogue.

The same manuscript contains poems copied by Taylor from Robert Wild and George Wither, demonstrating that "Taylor does not show discriminating literary taste. His chief preoccupations were theological and political. . . . The somewhat coarse satiric wit of Wild is echoed in Taylor's topical verses and in the speeches of Satan in *Gods Determinations*."

D. First Publication of Other Works

(Chronologically arranged)

33 "Dairy of Edward Taylor." *Massachusetts Historical Society Proceedings*, XVIII (1880), 5-18.

Excerpts in Lockwood, No. 73, I, 130-136; Sibley, No. 85, pp. 397-406; and *Westfield Jubilee*, No. 97, pp. 153-154. Entire diary reprinted in Murphy, No. 7. Dated April 26, 1668, to January 12, 1671/2. Describes Taylor's journey to New England, his life at Harvard, and his journey to Westfield. From the manuscript "Diary, Theological Notes and Poems" (No. 37).

34 Stanford, Donald E. "Edward Taylor's 'Spiritual Relation.'" *American Literature*, XXXV (1964), 467-475.

First publication (except for fragments in Lockwood, No. 73, I, 113-115), of Taylor's "Spiritual Relation," from the manuscript "The Publick Records of the Church at Westfield . . ."

Taylor's emphasis on sin in the "Relation" supports Stanford's argument against Kenneth Murdock (No. 122) and Perry Miller (Nos. 117, 119), who claim Taylor was not orthodox and lacked the acute sense of sin which his Puritan contemporaries had.

E. Manuscripts

Massachusetts Historical Society

35 ["Commonplace Book."] In the Massachusetts Historical Society. Presented by William P. Upham in 1900. About 400 pp.

Mainly Taylor's copies of various letters and pamphlets, some concerning him but most concerning issues of the day. Description of the manuscript in Stanford, No. 3, pp. 513-516.

Prince Library, Boston Public Library

36 "Extracts, by Reverend Edward Taylor, Westfield." In the Prince Library, Boston Public Library. Presented by the Deacons of the Old South Church, Boston. About 360 pp. by Taylor.

Includes material relating to Taylor's controversy with Solomon Stoddard—some original compositions by Taylor, and some copied by him from other writers. Among Taylor's own writings are "The Appeale Tried," erroneously attributed to Stoddard in the Prince Library Catalogue; "A Particular Church is God's House" (an expanded version of that in the manuscript "Publick Records of the Church at Westfield," No. 42); two sermons on the authority of the minister; and 8 sermons preached between about December 1693 and April 1694. Description of the manuscript in Grabo, No. 8, pp. liii-lvi and No. 188; and *The Prince Library: A Catalogue of the Collection of Books and Manuscripts . . . Now Deposited in the Public Library of the City of Boston* (Boston: A. Mudge and Son, 1870), p. 159.

Redwood Library and Athenaeum

37 ["Diary, Theological Notes, and Poems."] In the Redwood Library and Athenaeum at Newport, Rhode Island. Presented from the estate of Roderick Terry, Jr. in 1951. 146 unnumbered pp. (30 blank).

Includes Taylor's "Diary of Atlantic Voyage/Life at Harvard College/Settlement at Westfield, Mass./April 26, 1668—December 3, 1671"; "Theological Essays/1655"; and miscellaneous poems. Description of the manuscript in Stanford, No. 3, pp. 517-519.

38 ["Harmony of the Gospels."] In the Redwood Library and Athenaeum at Newport, Rhode Island. Presented from the estate of Roderick Terry, Jr. in 1951. 485 unnumbered pp.

A commentary on the gospels (incomplete), beginning with John 1:1 and ending with Matthew 12:24. Stiles' note in the manuscript judges the date to be about 1690-1710. Description of the manuscript in Stanford, No. 3, pp. 520-521.

39 ["A Metrical History of Christianity."] In the Redwood Library and Athenaeum at Newport, Rhode Island. Presented from the estate of Roderick Terry, Jr. in 1951. 438 pp. (4 blank).

Narrative poem in decasyllabic couplets, interspersed with verses of praise to God in various stanzaic patterns. Found in an attic in Enfield, Connecticut. Description of the manuscript in Stanford, No. 3, pp. 519-520; No. 5, pp. i-iii; and No. 261.

Westfield Athenaeum

40 "An Extract of the History of the Council of Trent." In the Westfield Athenaeum. Presented by Dr. Oliver Brewster Taylor in 1897. 312 pp.

Taylor's copy book of the "Extract" based on Nathaniel Brent's English translation of 1629. Description of the manuscript in Stanford, No. 3, p. 512; and Murphy, No. 241.

41 ["Origen's Contra Celsus and De Principiis."] In the Westfield Athenaeum. Presented by Dr. Oliver Brewster Taylor in 1897. About 500 pp.

Taylor's transcription of Origen's work. Description of the manuscript in Stanford, No. 3, p. 512; and Murphy, No. 241.

42 "The Publick Records of the Church at Westfield Together with a briefe account of our proceeding in order to our entrance into that state." In the Westfield Athenaeum. 308 pp. by Taylor (the manuscript continues the church record down to 1836).

Includes an account of Taylor's early years in Westfield, his "Spiritual Relation," the relations of the six foundation men, Taylor's ordination-day sermon "A Particular Church is God's House," and miscellaneous church records. Selections in Lockwood, No. 73, I, 107-119, 191-196, 218-230. Description of the manuscript in Stanford, No. 3, pp. 511-512.

Yale University Library

43 ["China's Description" and Commonplace Book.] In the Yale University Library. Presented by Henry Wyllys Taylor in 1883. About 335 pp. (28 blank).

Includes Taylor's transcription of a book by Louis Daniel Le Comte with Taylor's commentary following, and Taylor's commonplace book recording miracles and other strange phenomena. Description of the manuscript in Stanford, No. 3, p. 508.

44 "Christographia, or A Discourse toching Christs Person, Natures, the Personall Union of the Natures. Qualifications and Operations Opened, Confirmed, and Practically improoved in severall sermons delivered upon

Certain Sacrament Dayes unto the Church and people of God in Westfield." In the Yale University Library. Presented by Henry Wyllys Taylor in 1883. 340 pp.

Fourteen sermons on the nature of Christ, preached between August 26, 1701 and October 10, 1703. Description of the manuscript in Stanford, No. 3, pp. 509-511; and Grabo, No. 4, pp. xlv-xlviii.

45 ["Dispensatory."] In the Yale University Library. Presented by Henry Wyllys Taylor in 1883. About 500 pp.

Mainly descriptions of the medicinal properties of herbs, minerals, etc., extracted by Taylor from various seventeenth-century medical books. Description of the manuscript in Stanford, No. 3, p. 509, and Leighton, No. 110.

46 ["Manuscript Book."] In the Yale University Library. Presented by Henry Taylor Terry in 1921. 54 unnumbered pp. (18 blank).

Contains mostly drafts and versions of miscellaneous poems in the manuscript "Poetical Works." Description of the manuscript in Stanford, No. 3, pp. 506-508.

47 "Manuscript Notebook with Additional Annotations, by Isaac and Ezra Stiles." In the Yale University Library. Presented by Lewis Stiles Gannett in 1961.

A notebook in which Taylor had written theological headings, leaving space to annotate each one, though only a few have any annotations (mostly in Latin). Additional notes inserted on the blank pages by Isaac and Ezra Stiles. Description of the manuscript in Mignon, No. 233.

48 ["Metallographia."] In the Yale University Library. Presented by Henry Wyllys Taylor in 1883. 337 pp. (212 blank).

A few notes on Riverius' ". . . Principalls of Physick . . ." which Taylor had apparently intended to copy into the manuscript book. Most of the manuscript contains extracts from

John Webster's *Metallographia* (London, 1671), on the subject of "Gold, Philosophic Mercury and Transmutation." Description of the manuscript in Stanford, No. 3, pp. 508-509.

49 ["Poetical Works."] In the Yale University Library. Presented by Henry Wyllys Taylor in 1868. 400 pp.

Contains the bulk of Taylor's poetry, including elegies, his college declamation, love letter to Elizabeth Fitch, miscellaneous poems, "Description of the great Bones dug up at Clavarack," *Gods Determinations*, "Prologue," and the *Preparatory Meditations*. Description of the manuscript in Johnson, No. 1, pp. 221-228; and Stanford, No. 3, pp. 502-506.

50 [Poems Found in the Binding of the "Poetical Works" Manuscript.] In the Yale University Library. 82 pp.

Includes copies of *Preparatory Meditations* 1.1-8, the first two stanzas of 1.9, "The Experience," "The Return," and "The Reflexion," as well as metrical paraphrases of some Biblical passages. Description of the manuscript in Stanford, No. 3, p. 506.

For further discussion related to Taylor's manuscripts see Johnson, No. 1, pp. 229-231 and Mignon, No. 237.

II. Secondary Sources

F. Bibliographies

(Chronologically arranged)

51 Hoffman, Carol Ann. "Edward Taylor: A Selected Bibliography." *Bulletin of Bibliography*, XXIII (1961), 85-87.

A fairly complete listing of critical articles to 1961, but no biographical sources or reviews.

52 Elkins, Mary Jane. "Edward Taylor: A Checklist." *Early American Literature*, IV, No. 1 (1969), 56-63.

Chronological arrangement. Brings Hoffmann up to date through 1969.

53 Requa, Kenneth A., Karl Keller, and Everett H. Emerson. "Additions to the Edward Taylor Checklist." *Early American Literature*, IV, No. 3 (1969–70), 117-119.

54 Scheick, William J. "More Additions to the Edward Taylor Checklist." *Early American Literature*, V, No. 2 (1970), 62.

G. Biography and Genealogy

55 Anonymous. "A Historical Sketch of Stoddardeanism, with some account of its effect on the churches in Old Hampshire County, Mass." *The New Englander*, IV (1846), 354.

A brief mention of the decision of the Westfield church to accept "Stoddardeanism."

56 Caulkins, Frances M. *History of Norwich, Connecticut from Its Possession by the Indians to the Year 1866*. Hartford: By the Author, 1866, pp. 151, 153, 155, 337.

Includes Taylor's love letter to Elizabeth Fitch (No. 10).

57 Connecticut Colony. *The Public Records of the Colony of Connecticut* [1636–1776]. Ed. James H. Trumbull (vols. I-III) and C. J. Headly (vols. IV-XV). Hartford: Press of the Case, Lockwood and Brainerd Company, 1850–1890. II, 431; IV, 383.

Includes summary of letter to the Boston Council (No. 13).

58 Davis, Emerson. "Descendants of Rev. Edward Taylor of Westfield, Mass." *New England Historical and Genealogical Register*, II (1848), 395.

59 ———. *A Historical Sketch of Westfield*. Westfield, Mass.: J. Root, 1826, pp. 7, 28-29.

Includes excerpts from Taylor's description of King Philip's War (p. 7), as well as a biographical sketch of Taylor (pp. 28-29).

60 ———. "A Record of Marriages, Births, and Deaths in Westfield, Mass., Prior to the Year 1700." *New England Historical and Genealogical Register*, VI (1852), 267.

61 Dexter, Franklin B. *Biographical Sketches of the Graduates of Yale College*. New York: Henry Holt and Company, 1885–1912. I–III, *passim*.

62 Dickinson, James Taylor. *Genealogies of the Lymans of Middlefield, of the Dickinsons of Montreal, and of the Partridges of Hatfield*. Boston: D. Clapp and Son, Printers, 1865, pp. 22, 24.

63 Edwards, B. B. "Complete List of the Congregational Ministers in the Old County of Hampshire, Ms. . . ." *American Quarterly Register*, X (1838), 384, 401.

64 Farmer, John. *A Genealogical Register of the First Settlers of New England*. Lancaster, Massachusetts: Carter, Andrews and Company, 1829; Baltimore: Genealogical Publishing Co., 1969, p. 282.

65 Greenough, J. C. "Historical Relation of Springfield and Westfield." *Connecticut Valley Historical Society Papers and Proceedings*, II (1904), 252-263, *passim*.

66 Hampshire County, Mass. "Inventory of the Estate of the Reverend Edward Taylor, January 13, 1729/30." Northampton Probate Records, V.

The full inventory is transcribed by Lockwood in No. 72, pp. 42-44.

67 Holland, Josiah G. *History of Western Massachusetts*. Springfield, Massachusetts: S. Bowles and Company, 1855. I, 66, 107-108, 115-118; II, 141-144.

68 Holmes, Abiel. *The Life of Ezra Stiles*. Boston: Thomas and Andrews, 1798, p. 381.

69 Johnson, Thomas H. "Edward Taylor." *Dictionary of American Biography*. Ed. Harris E. Starr. Supplement I. New York: Charles Scribner's Sons, 1944, pp. 681-682.

70 Judd Manuscripts. Forbes Library, Northampton, Massachusetts. II, 215.

71 "A List of Gravestones in the Mechanic Street Cemetery, Westfield, Massachusetts, 1939." Typescript in the Westfield Athenaeum, Westfield, Mass., 1939, p. 184.

Text of Taylor's gravestone in Terry, No. 95, p. 25 and Lockwood, No. 72, p. 18.

72 Lockwood, John Hoyt. *A Sermon Commemorative of the Two-Hundredth Anniversary of the First Congregational Church of Westfield, Mass., Delivered by the Pastor, Rev. John H. Lockwood, Sunday, Oct. 5, 1879*. Westfield, Mass.: Clark and Story, Printers, 1879, pp. 9-20, 33-34, 37-44.

Includes transcription of Taylor's tombstone (No. 71), the "Letter to the Churches . . ." (No. 15), Taylor's love letter to Elizabeth Fitch (No. 10), the inventory of Taylor's estate (No. 66), and Taylor's transcription of the formal commission from the governor and assistants to organize the Westfield church.

73 ———. *Westfield and Its Historic Influences, 1669–1919 . . .* Springfield, Massachusetts: By the Author, 1922. I, 102-321, *passim*.

Includes transcripts of several of Taylor's letters (Nos. 10, 11, 12, 13, 15), excerpts from Taylor's Diary (Nos. 7, 33), and excerpts from his "Spiritual Relation" (No. 34), and other parts of the Westfield Church Record.

74 Medlicott, Alexander, Jr. "Notes on Edward Taylor from the Diaries of Stephen Williams." *American Literature*, XXXIV (1962), 270-274.

75 Morison, Samuel Eliot. *Harvard College in the Seventeenth Century*. Cambridge: Harvard University Press, 1936. I, 83, 85, 124, 143, 233; II, 558.

76 Nason, Emma C. "Ruth Taylor and her Five Daughters," and "More About Ruth Taylor, Her Ancestors, and Descendants." In Terry, No. 95, pp. 27-80.

Sketches of Ruth Taylor, her influence on her children, and her children's influence on subsequent descendants. Some fanciful story-telling, but most is historically sound.

77 [Obituary.] *Boston News-Letter*, August 7–14, 1729, p. [2].

Includes a brief biographical sketch of Taylor.

78 [Obituary.] *New England Weekly Journal*, July 14, 1729, p. [2].

79 Paige, Lucius R. "List of Freemen." *New England Historical and Genealogical Register*, III (1849), 245.

80 Perkins, Fred B. "Perkins Family of Connecticut." *New England Historical and Genealogical Register*, XV (1861), 117.

81 Savage, James. *A Genealogical Dictionary of the First Settlers of New England, Showing Three Generations of Those Who Came before May, 1692, on the Basis of Farmer's Register*. [See No. 64.] Boston: Little, Brown and Company, 1860–1862. II, 168; IV, 259.

82 Sewall, Samuel. *Diary of Samuel Sewall, 1674–1729. Massachusetts Historical Society Collections*. Fifth Series, V, 6–VII, 389, *passim*.

References to Taylor begin on November 5, 1674, with mention of his wedding and continue to December 22, 1727, about a year before his death.

83 ———. *Letter-Book of Samuel Sewall [1685–1729]. Massachusetts Historical Society Collections*. Sixth Series. I, 88–II, 274, *passim*.

84 Sheldon, George. *A History of Deerfield, Massachusetts*. Deerfield: E. A. Hall and Company, 1895. II, Part 2, 334.

85 Sibley, John L. *Biographical Sketches of Graduates of Harvard University* . . . Cambridge: Harvard University Press, 1873–1885. II, 397-412, 534-536.

Based largely on Sprague (Nos. 90, 92). Includes letters of Henry W. Taylor and quotations from Ezra Stiles. Together with Sprague, largely responsible for the myth that Taylor's supposed will included an injunction against publication. Includes excerpts from Taylor's Diary (Nos. 7, 33).

86 Stanford, Donald E. "The Parentage of Edward Taylor." *American Literature*, XXXIII (1961), 215-221.

Contains transcripts of the wills of William Taylor of Sketchley (d. 1658), Taylor's father, and of Richard Taylor of Sketchley (d. 1689), Taylor's oldest brother.

87 Stiles, Ezra. *Extracts from the Itineraries and other Miscellanies of Ezra Stiles*. Ed. Franklin B. Dexter. New Haven: Yale University Press, 1916. VI, 81-83, 89, 198, 203-204, 206, 277, 403-404.

88 ———. Folio Manuscripts. Yale University Library. pp. 73-76.

89 ———. *The Literary Diary of Ezra Stiles*. Ed. Franklin B. Dexter. New York: Charles Scribner's Sons, 1901. I, 367-368, 485.

90 ———. "Memoir of Rev'd Mr. Taylor [May 8, 1767]." *Annals of the American Pulpit*. Ed. William B. Sprague. New York: R. Carter and Brothers, 1857–1859. I, 181.

A memoir which Stiles had written in Taylor's manuscript "Metallographia" (No. 48), transcribed by Henry Wyllys Taylor and included in his letter to Sprague. (See H. W. Taylor, No. 92). Reprinted in Mignon, No. 237.

91 Talcott, Mary K. "The Wyllys Family of Connecticut." *New England Historical and Genealogical Register*, XXXVII (1883), 34.

92 Taylor, Henry Wyllys. [Letter to William Sprague, September 18, 1851.] *Annals of the American Pulpit*. Ed. William B. Sprague. New York: R. Carter and Brothers, 1857–1859, I, 177-181.

Partially reprinted in *Westfield Jubilee*, No. 97, pp. 152-155. Contains H. W. Taylor's transcription of Ezra Stiles "Memoir" of Edward Taylor. (See Stiles, No. 90.)

93 ———. [Letters of November 30 and December 13, 1880, and January 19, 1881.] Extracts in Sibley, No. 85, 535-536.

94 Terry, John T[aylor]. "Religious Influences in American Civilization—Its Founders." *Journal of American History*, V (1911), 129-135.

Biographical and genealogical sketch of Taylor from Terry's own investigation. Includes Taylor's love letter to Elizabeth Fitch (No. 10), and extracts from Taylor's diary (Nos. 7, 33).

"It is sometimes said that the old New England Puritans had no poetry in them, but I think that this letter, with its drawings of a heart, ring and dove, rather tends to disprove such an assertion."

95 ———. *Rev. Edward Taylor, 1642–1729*. New York: Privately Printed by the DeVinne Press, 1892.

A biographical sketch of Taylor, drawing on his own diary, on Stiles, and on Lockwood. Includes love letter to Elizabeth Fitch (No. 10), and the text of Taylor's gravestone (No. 71). The last two-thirds of the book is taken up with two sketches by Emma C. Nason (No. 76).

96 Walworth, Reuben H. *Hyde Genealogy*. Albany: J. Munsell, 1864. I, 285-286; II, 1173.

97 *The Westfield Jubilee: A Report of the Celebration at Westfield, Mass. on the Two Hundredth Anniversary of the Incorporation of the Town, October 6, 1869, With the Historical Address of the Hon. William G. Bates . . .*

Westfield, Mass.: Clark and Story, Publishers, 1870, 56-63, 125-126, 152-159.

Includes Taylor's love letter to Elizabeth Fitch (No. 10), the letter to the Boston Council (No. 13), and excerpts from Taylor's Diary (Nos. 7, 33).

H. Critical Books

98 Grabo, Norman S. *Edward Taylor.* Twayne's United States Authors Series, No. 8. New Haven: College and University Press, 1961. 192 pp.

This first book-length treatment of Taylor emphasizes the mystical aspects of his poetry. Reading his *Preparatory Meditations* helps to correct the distorted view of Puritanism as dark and somber, and to emphasize the devotional, contemplative side. Taylor's main purpose was the imitation of Christ, both as teacher and as artist; "his mysticism made him publicly a preacher just as it made him privately a poet."

Taylor's success as a poet, however, is limited because the basis of his poetry is largely ornamentation, and "Taylor frankly views it as a mode of decorating the transcendent truths of his faith." His development as a poet was impeded not because of his theology, however, but because, like most Puritan writers, he accepted the teaching of Ramus "that rhetoric itself is the dressing of oratory and that poetry is the 'tricking out' of that dressing."

Grabo argues that the *Preparatory Meditations* are better than *Gods Determinations* because the weakness of Taylor's versification is excusable in poems in which "personal piety rather than poetry is the main end but in which they coalesce frequently enough to succeed beautifully." In *Gods Determinations*, on the other hand, "imaginative and didactic purposes cross too frequently, and tempt Taylor into unpardonable preachiness."

Reviewed in Nos. 143, 172, 259, 263, 280.

99 Nicolaisen, Peter. *Die Bildlichkeit in der Dichtung Edward Taylors.* Kieler Beiträge zur Anglistik und Amerikanistik 4. Neumünster: Karl Wachholtz Verlag, 1966. 179 pp.

A revision of the author's doctoral dissertation (No. 298). Includes an "English Summary," pp. 175-179. Examines the relationship between Taylor's imagery and the theological and historical background of his poetry. Shows how the sources of Taylor's images were more often Biblical than personal, especially as he grew older and became more dependent on scripture.

Prefers the typological poems among the *Preparatory Meditations* because they are more concrete, more "real." Likewise argues that the images in *Gods Determinations* are "much more tangible and are transposed into the poet's own world much more strikingly than the subject matter of the *Meditations*."

Reviewed in Nos. 193, 247a.

100 Stanford, Donald E. *Edward Taylor*. University of Minnesota Pamphlets on American Writers, No. 52. Minneapolis: University of Minnesota Press, 1965. 46 pp.

A general introduction to Taylor and his poetry, reflecting Stanford's emphasis on his orthodoxy. Concludes that while his work ranks below the achievement of the English Metaphysicals, there is still an "impressive body of poetry" on the whole.

Reviewed in Nos. 144, 178, and 180.

I. Critical Articles in Books

101 Abel, Darrel. "Edward Taylor." *American Literature: I. Colonial and Early National Writing.* Woodbury, N. Y.: Barron's Educational Series, Inc., 1963, pp. 86-91.

A not entirely reliable discussion of Taylor (e.g., Abel mistakenly says that none of Taylor's sermons are extant). Feels that "Taylor's poetry is the finest esthetic flowering of the Puritan sensibility" and discusses it largely in terms of his "metrical versatility" and "verbal resourcefulness."

102 Altick, Richard D. *The Scholar Adventurers.* New York: Macmillan, 1950, 306-308.

A discussion of Johnson's "discovery" of Taylor's poems.

103 Benét, William Rose and Norman Holmes Pearson, eds. "Edward Taylor." *Oxford Anthology of American Literature.* New York: Oxford University Press, 1938. I, 60-63.

The first anthology to include poems by Taylor: "Prologue"; part of "Preface" and all of "The Joy of Church Fellowship" from *Gods Determinations*; and Meditations 1.1, 3, and 38 are all reprinted from Johnson (No. 20).

Prefatory discussion partially reprinted in Adams, No. 137, p. 101. A general introduction of Taylor to readers of American poetry. Compares him with the English Metaphysicals. "He is a lesser Crashaw or Herbert, but he is a true poet."

104 Brumm, Ursula. "Edward Taylors Meditationen über das Abendmahl." *Die Religiöse Typologie im amerikanischen*

Denken. Studien zür amerikanischer Literature und Geschichte, 2. Leiden: Brill, 1963, pp. 49-72.

English translation in No. 105. An important book, which shows how "the theory and practice of symbolism in the American classics developed out of Puritan forms of thought and belief," especially of typology. Edward Taylor's use of allegory is an example of the way symbolism began to grow out of Puritan typology, even though theoretically the Puritans rejected symbolism. Taylor's "absolute spiritualization of all images far surpasses what the Puritans considered theologically permissible," but it "stems from tendencies and problems inherent in Puritan theology."

105 ———. "Edward Taylor's Meditations on the Lord's Supper." *American Thought and Religious Typology*. Trans. John Hoaglund. New Brunswick, N. J.: Rutgers University Press, 1970, pp. 56-85.

A translation of No. 104.

106 Faust, C. H. "The Decline of Puritanism." *Transitions in American Literary History*. Ed. Harry Hayden Clark. Durham, N. C.: Duke University Press, 1953, pp. 11, 14-16.

A brief comparison of *Gods Determinations* with Wigglesworth's *Day of Doom*. Argues that *Gods Determinations*, with its emphasis on grace and love, shows a truer picture of the Puritan God than does Wigglesworth's poem with its emphasis on damnation.

107 Grant, Douglas. "Edward Taylor: Poet in a Wilderness." *Purpose and Place: Essays on American Writers*. London: The Macmillan Company; New York: St. Martin's Press. 1965, pp. 7-13.

Largely a reprint of No. 198.

108 Jantz, Harold Stein. *The First Century of New England Verse*. New York: Russell and Russell, 1962, pp. 79-85, 262-263.

First published in 1943 (*American Antiquarian Society Proceedings*, LIII, 219-523), Jantz is the first to include Taylor in a general study of colonial literature. Believes Taylor's genius "lies in his remarkable ability to infuse abstract concepts, even theological dogmas, with the pulsating breath of life." He "domesticates" his ideas with images from everyday life and therefore "does not generally provide a poetic incarnation on the same exalted level which the ideas occupy." But if his poetry is not so lofty as the great English Metaphysicals, it is more typically American.

109 Krishnamurthi, M. G. "Edward Taylor: A Note on the American Literary Tradition." *Indian Essays in American Literature: Papers in Honor of Robert E. Spiller*. Ed. Sujit Mukherjee and D. U. K. Raghavacharyulu. Bombay: Popular Prakashan, 1969, pp. 27-39.

110 Leighton, Ann. *Early American Gardens: For Meate or Medicine*. Boston: Houghton-Mifflin, 1970, pp. 115-116; 222-223.

Describes Taylor's manuscript "Dispensatory" (No. 45) and briefly discusses his interest in gardening, alchemy, astrology, and medicine.

110a Lenhart, Charmenz S. *Musical Influences on American Poetry*. Athens, Ga.: University of Georgia Press, 1956, pp. 45-53.

Discusses the musical influences on Taylor's conceits. Although his poems are too weighty and their meter too rough to call them lyrical, it is clear that "music played an important part in his creative thinking."

111 Ludwig, Allan I. *Graven Images: New England Stonecarving and Its Symbols, 1650–1815*. Middletown, Conn.: Wesleyan University Press, 1966, *passim*.

A fascinating study of Puritan uses of emblems and symbols, using Taylor's poems (among many other sources) to illuminate the stonecarving.

112 Lynen, John F. "Literary Form and the Design of Puritan Experience." *The Design of the Present: Essays on Time and Form in American Literature.* New Haven and London: Yale University Press, 1969, pp. 49-51, 61-70, 72-73.

Because of the typically Puritan way of perceiving time through a sharp contrast between present and eternity, Taylor was unable to carry a metaphor beyond the level of analogy or sign to the level of conceit or symbol, to achieve the "perfect fusion of vehicle and tenor" that Donne could. But in *Gods Determinations,* Taylor's use of a series of static "moments" anticipates "the rather special ways of manipulating time which would become characteristic of American Literature."

113 Martz, Louis. "Edward Taylor: *Preparatory Meditations.*" *The Poem of the Mind: Essays on Poetry, English and American.* New York: Oxford University Press, 1966, pp. 54-81.

Largely a reprint of his "Foreword" to the Stanford edition of Taylor's poems (No. 114).

114 ———. "Foreword." *The Poems of Edward Taylor.* Ed. Donald E. Stanford, No. 3, pp. xii-xxxvii.

Revised and reprinted in No. 113.

An important essay which sets the tone for subsequent Taylor criticism in several ways. Puts Taylor in the tradition of "meditative" poets and shows limitations of considering him only a "metaphysical" poet. Argues that Taylor's poetic reputation must stand or fall on the *Preparatory Meditations,* not on *Gods Determinations,* as Johnson had argued. Shows how the American wilderness resulted in a lack of cultural feedback; it was a nonartistic environment, not an anti-artistic one as so many critics had argued. Shows how Taylor helped to mark the beginnings of an American language and an American literature.

115 Meserole, Harrison T., ed. "Edward Taylor." *Seventeenth-Century American Poetry*. Garden City, N. Y.: Doubleday and Company, 1968, pp. 119-123.

A general introduction to Taylor's poetry; he "achieved a level of poetic art which remained unequaled in America until the beginning of the nineteenth century."

116 Miller, Perry, ed. *The American Puritans: Their Poetry and Prose*. New York: Doubleday and Company (Anchor paperback A80), 1956, pp. 301-303, 309.

Discusses Taylor's "secret" writing of poetry: he was an orthodox Puritan in regard to federal theology, but wrote poems which he preferred not to publish.

117 ———. *The New England Mind: From Colony to Province*. Cambridge: Harvard University Press, 1953; Boston: The Beacon Press, 1961, pp. 155, 240, 284.

Brief mention of the unorthodox nature of Taylor's sensuous images, important because of the critical reactions it caused. Brief discussion of Taylor's quarrel with Stoddard.

118 ———. *The New England Mind: The Seventeenth Century*. New York: The Macmillan Company, 1939; Cambridge: Harvard University Press, 1954; Boston: Beacon Press, 1961, pp. 327, 361.

Brief discussion of Taylor in relation to Puritan rhetoric.

119 ———, and Thomas H. Johnson, eds. *The Puritans: A Sourcebook of Their Writings*. Rev. ed. New York: Harper and Row, 1963. II, 650-652.

Emphasizes Taylor's unorthodox metaphysical poetry, which "overleaped the limits of the doctrines he professed" and which accounts for "his injunction that his heirs should never publish his verses." Cf. Stanford, Nos. 132, 260.

120 Morison, Samuel Eliot. *The Intellectual Life of Colonial New England*. 2nd ed. New York: New York University Press, 1956, pp. 235-240.

The *Preparatory Meditations* "owe their style as well as their conception to George Herbert; they are a continuous outpouring of the author's love for God." Affirms Taylor's orthodoxy. "There was nothing unusual, for a New England puritan clergyman, in Taylor's sweet inner life or in his fervid adoration of his Saviour. The uncommon thing about him is his expression of it."

121 Murdock, Kenneth. "The Colonial and Revolutionary Period." Part I of *The Literature of the American People, an Historical and Critical Survey*. Ed. Arthur Hobson Quinn. New York: Appleton-Century-Crofts, 1951, p. 57.

Murdock here emphasizes Taylor's unorthodoxy as a Puritan, which he discusses at more length in No. 122.

122 ———. "A Little Recreation of Poetry." *Literature and Theology in Colonial New England*. Cambridge: Harvard University Press, 1949; New York: Harper and Row (Harper Torchbook, TB/99), 1963, pp. 152-171.

While Taylor's poetry differs from that of the English Metaphysicals because of his Puritan theology, it is "not typical of New England Puritan poetry, because it is richer in insight and more expert in technique." Taylor's poetic soul and religious raptures often led him beyond the bounds of orthodoxy in using sensuous imagery. The two important qualities in his poetry are an earthy realism in diction and imagery, and his use of the tones of speech.

123 ———. "Writers of New England." *Literary History of the United States*. Ed. Robert E. Spiller *et al*. 3rd. ed., rev. New York: The Macmillan Company; London: Collier-Macmillan Limited, 1963, pp. 65-68.

An enthusiastic discussion of Taylor's poetry. The sensuousness and mysticism of his poems, while beyond the bounds of Puritan orthodoxy and probably the cause of his injunction not to publish, together with his use of realistic and homely imagery create an effective sense of dramatic tension. "Again and again he makes articulate the drama inherent in man's quest for a beauty which is beyond earth but realizable only in images of earthly delights."

124 Ong, Walter S., S. J. *Ramus: Method, and the Decay of Dialogue: From the Art of Discourse to the Art of Reason.* Cambridge: Harvard University Press, 1958, p. 287.

A brief discussion of Taylor, but important because of the critical comment it has elicited. In general the New England Puritans based their theories of poetry on Ramist rhetoric, emphasizing didactic monologue rather than dialogue (cf. their dislike of drama). In contrast Taylor, "the one New England Puritan who wrote poetry derivative from the Elizabethan dramatic experience, is the least Puritan and least Ramistic of all New England writers."

125 Pearce, Roy Harvey. "Edward Taylor: The Poet as Puritan." *Critical Approaches to American Literature.* Ed. Ray B. Browne and Martin Light. New York: Thomas Y. Crowell Company, 1965. I, 13-25.

A reprint of No. 244.

126 ———. "Taylor." *The Continuity of American Poetry.* Princeton: Princeton University Press, 1961, pp. 42-54.

Partially a revision of No. 244. Taylor exhibits the characteristically Puritan belief that poetry cannot be written without Grace; hence the conflict between "his natural desire to 'make' poems and his knowledge that, as a natural man, he had neither the right nor the power to 'make' anything." Taylor believed, as a Puritan, that Art must be subservient to Nature, and both to God; yet for that reason he was able to find an " 'artless' art, one which in the hands of a master like him is art indeed."

127 Piercy, Josephine K. *Studies in Literary Types in Seventeenth-Century America, 1607–1710*. New Haven: Yale University Press; London: Oxford University Press, 1939, p. 37.

A brief discussion of Taylor not as a poet, but as a student of science. Apparently the author was not yet aware of Johnson's first publication of Taylor's poems (No. 20), and so this discussion is important for historical rather than critical reasons. She notes that Taylor transcribed Riviere's "Principles of Physic" (No. 48) and mentions another manuscript on scientific matters (No. 45), concluding that "apparently there were no religious scruples against scientific study among the divines."

128 Pope, Robert G. *The Half-Way Covenant: Church Membership in Puritan New England*. Princeton, N. J.: Princeton University Press, 1969, pp. 190-191, 254-255.

A brief discussion of Taylor in the context of Puritan controversies over church membership.

129 Schulze, Fritz W. "Strophe, Vers und Reim in Edward Taylors *Meditations*." *Literatur und Sprache der Vereinigten Staaten: Aufsätze zu Ehren von Hans Galinsky*. Ed. Hans Helmcke, Klaus Lubbers, and Renate Schmidt-von Bardeleben. Heidelberg: Winter Verlag, 1969, pp. 11-33.

130 Shea, Daniel B. "Edward Taylor's 'Spiritual Relation.' " *Spiritual Autobiography in Early America*. Princeton: Princeton University Press, 1968, pp. 92-100.

Although the discovery of Taylor's poetry "revealed unsuspected dimensions in the Puritan aesthetic," his "Spiritual Relation" is completely conventional, as the genre tended to be, "a textbook conversion which allows only a fleeting glimpse of the rich meditative life regularly encountered in his poetry."

131 Silverman, Kenneth, ed. "Edward Taylor." *Colonial American Poetry*. New York: Hafner Publishing Company, 1968, pp. 173-179.

Taylor is the epitome of the Puritan doctrinal poet, "whose work seldom yields large humanistic propositions." The diction in his poetry is "a spectacularly discordant array of scholastic terminology, dialect, coinages and colloquialisms."

132 Stanford, Donald E. "The Puritan Poet as Preacher: An Edward Taylor Sermon." *Studies in American Literature*. Ed. Waldo McNeir and Leo B. Levy. Louisiana State University Studies, Humanities Series No. 8. Baton Rouge: Louisiana State University Press, 1960, pp. 1-10.

Continuing his defense of Taylor's orthodoxy, Stanford discusses Sermon 10 from *Christographia* (see also No. 260). Taylor is a rigidly dogmatic predestinarian, not a univeralist as the Glossary of Johnson's edition of Taylor's poems (No. 1) would indicate. Taylor's poetry is successful because of, not in spite of, his Calvinism, for it reflects the joy of his being among the elect.

133 Waggoner, Hyatt H. "Edward Taylor." *American Poets: From the Puritans to the Present*. Boston: Houghton-Mifflin Company, 1968, pp. 16-24.

Taylor is better seen as a forerunner of Emerson than as the end of the metaphysical school. Because of his Puritan theology, his poetry is often bigoted, metaphorically incoherent, and lacking in the tension between attachment to the world and detachment which is characteristic of all great religious poetry.

134 Warren, Austin. "Edward Taylor." *Major Writers of America*. Ed. Perry Miller, et al. New York: Harcourt, Brace and World, 1962. I, pp. 51-62.

A full appreciation of Taylor cannot come through reading anthology selections, but by reading him whole. His work is uneven, and "it is the persistence of his literary-spiritual endeavor to discover and celebrate 'ultimate reality' which is more impressive than any single poem or selection of poems." Discusses the American aspects of Taylor's poetry; his isolation is what makes him most distinctively American.

135 ———. "Edward Taylor." *Rage for Order*. Ann Arbor: University of Michigan Press, 1948, pp. 1-18.

A revised version of No. 273.

135a Whicher, George F. "Parson Taylor of Westfield." *Mornings at 8:50: Brief Evocations of the Past for a College Audience*. Northampton, Mass.: Published by the Hampshire Bookshop for the Trustees of Amherst College, 1950, pp. 121-126.

A brief sketch of Taylor's life and writings, originally given as a chapel talk at Amherst College.

136 Wright, Thomas Goddard. *Literary Culture in Early New England 1620–1730*. New Haven: Yale University Press, 1920, pp. 136*n*, 162.

The only comment about Taylor as a poet between Sprague (Nos. 90, 92) and Johnson (No. 20). In discussing the dearth of literature in early New England, mentions that "Edward Taylor of Westfield filled a notebook with verse, none of which has ever been published, as the writer forbade publication."

J. Critical Articles in Periodicals

137 Adams, Frederick B. "The Crow's Nest." *Colophon*, New Graphic Series, I, No. 2 (1939), 100-106.

A favorable review of *The Poetical Works* (Johnson, No. 1). Includes another review by Stanley T. Williams (No. 279) and "The Discovery of Edward Taylor's Poetry" by Thomas Johnson (No. 211).

138 Akiyama, Ken. "Edward Taylor's Poetry: An Introduction" [in Japanese]. *Studies in Humanities* [Osaka], LXIV (1963), 27-44.

139 Alexis, Gerhard T. "A Keen Nose for Taylor's Syntax." *Early American Literature*, IV, No. 3 (1969-70), 97-101.

An explication of a difficult passage in the second "Christ's Reply" in *Gods Determinations*.

140 ———. "Taylor's 'Meditation 8.'" *Explicator*, XXIV (1966), Item 77.

The difficulty of the first four lines disappears when "divine" is read as a verb and "ly" as an infinitive.

140a Allen, Judson Boyce. "Edward Taylor's Catholic Wasp: Exegetical Convention in 'Upon a Spider Catching a Fly.'" *English Language Notes*, VII (1970), 257-260.

Contrary to Stanford's opinion (No. 100) that Taylor's choice of images is arbitrary, the spider, wasp, and fly have precedents in medieval Latin commentaries on the Bible. Demonstrates the strict logical structure of the poem according to the old exegetical tradition.

141 Anonymous. "More than Enough There: The Recognition of American Literature in England." *Times Literary Supplement*, LVIII (Special Supplement, November 6, 1959), xiv-xv.

Argues for the need to consider American literature independently of the English tradition. Edward Taylor's world is one of blacks and whites, while George Herbert, for instance, is more sensitive to the nuances of human nature. Nevertheless, even in the early stages of American literature there exists, "along with the crudeness and dullness of much of the verse, a certain felicity of tone which arises from the homely imagery and the forthright attitude of mind."

142 Anonymous. "The Muse." *Saturday Review*, June 11, 1966, p. 57.

A generally favorable review of Johnson's 1966 edition of *The Poetical Works* (No. 9), but does not recognize it as a new edition.

143 Anonymous. [Review] *Booklist*, LVIII (1962), 518.

A favorable review of Grabo's *Edward Taylor* (No. 98).

144 Anonymous. [Review] *Choice*, III (1966), 523.

A brief favorable review of Stanford's *Edward Taylor* (No. 100).

145 Anonymous [Review] *Choice*, III (1966), 802.

A brief review of the *Treatise Concerning the Lord's Supper* (Grabo, No. 8).

146 Anonymous. [Review] *New Republic*, C (1939), 321.

A brief, generally favorable review of *The Poetical Works* (Johnson, No. 1).

147 Anonymous. [Review] *New Yorker*, October 29, 1960, pp. 187-188.

A favorable review of *The Poems* (Stanford, No. 3).

148 Anonymous. [Review] *Times Literary Supplement*, LXII (1963), 674.

A review of *Christographia* (Grabo, No. 4). Grabo shows that while Taylor's subject was not unusual, he was original in "his comparative optimism and exultancy in arguing from Christ that man was not as depraved as Calvinism commonly insisted."

149 Arner, Robert D. "Edward Taylor's Gaming Imagery: 'Meditation 1.40.' " *Early American Literature*, IV, No. 1 (1969), 38-40.

Discusses sexual puns on the games and shows how they act as a compressing device "to concentrate several sins into one word" and thus emphasize the theme of man's depravity and God's grace.

150 Bach, Bert C. "Self Depreciation [sic] in Edward Taylor's *Sacramental Meditations*." *Cithara*, VI, No. 1 (1966), 49-59.

The common structural pattern of "statement of self-deprecation—plea for grace—realization of grace" which is reflected in images of dark and light and in figures of illness and healing, demonstrates Taylor's orthodox Puritanism.

151 Bales, Kent and William J. Aull. "Touching Taylor Overly: A Note on 'Meditation Six.' " *Early American Literature*, V, No. 2 (1970), 57-59.

Clarifies the meaning of the first stanza of Meditation 6 by demonstrating that "overly" in the last line means "superficially."

152 Ball, Kenneth R. "Rhetoric in Edward Taylor's *Preparatory Meditations*." *Early American Literature*, IV, No. 3 (1969–70), 79-88.

Taylor uses the traditional rhetorical figures amplification and meieosis to enhance and diminish, for instance, God's glory and man's worthiness. Thus the seemingly discordant images meaningfully reinforce Taylor's themes.

153 Ballinger, Martha. "The Metaphysical Echo." *English Studies in Africa*, VIII (1965), 71-80.

A vague and undefined concept of metaphysical leads Ballinger to see it as a "dominant gene" in American literature—from Edward Taylor to Elinor Wylie, Hawthorne, and Melville.

154 Benton, Robert M. "Edward Taylor's Use of His Text." *American Literature*, XXXIX (1967), 31-41.

Takes issue with Grabo (No. 4, pp. xxxiv-xliii) that the Meditations are based on the "doctrine" of the sermon. Instead, Benton argues "that the texts form the basis of the sermons and, in a parallel but independent manner, the basis of the poems."

155 Black, Mindele. "Edward Taylor: Heaven's Sugar Cake." *New England Quarterly*, XXIX (1956), 159-181.

The seemingly discordant images and tone in Taylor's poems can be explained by a split in Protestant, and especially Puritan, theology—the conflict between Christ as Judge and Christ as Love. In his sermons Taylor emphasizes the sterner aspects of Calvinistic theology, while in the Meditations he is very close to the feeling and expression of Anglo-Catholic and Roman Catholic baroque devotional literature. This split causes incongruity in his images, "a kind of aesthetic schizophrenia" in which household terms are side by side with Calvinistic theological terms. The result is sometimes charming, but the overall effect "is bound to be uneven, and this is the most frequent criticism made of Taylor's poetry."

156 Blake, Howard. "Seventeenth-Century Yankee." *Poetry*, LVI (1940), 165-169.

A generally favorable review of *The Poetical Works* (Johnson, No. 1), but disagrees with some of Johnson's choices of poems and with his belief that Taylor is most like Crashaw. "One should not seek in him verse superior to Quarles', but one may well find in him agreeable variations on a signal style of English poetry."

157 Blau, Herbert. "Heaven's Sugar Cake: Theology and Imagery in the Poetry of Edward Taylor." *New England Quarterly*, XXVI (1953), 337-360.

Emphasizes the incongruity between Taylor's metaphysicality and his Puritanism. Believes Taylor is unorthodox, because his rapturous joy at the Sacrament is inconsistent in a Calvinist who does not believe in the Real Presence, and because in *Gods Determinations* there is too much emphasis on repentence for a believer in predestination. (See Stanford, No. 260, for an answer.)

158 Bottorff, William K. "Edward Taylor: An Explication: 'Another Meditation at the Same Time.' " *Early American Literature*, III, No. 1 (1968), 17-21.

Meditation 1.6 is one of Taylor's finest because the extended conceit of the speaker's soul as the Lord's gold coin makes the poem one of his most unified.

159 Brown, Wallace C. "Edward Taylor: An American 'Metaphysical.' " *American Literature,* XVI (1944), 186-197.

Prefers "metaphysical" to "baroque" as a description of Taylor's poetry, which does not use imagery merely decoratively but organically in a tightly logical structure (cf. Warren, No. 273). The shock or surprise which results from "domesticating the infinite" often offends decorum, and emphasizes the differences rather than the similarities. But as his best Taylor achieves the "sensuous apprehension of thought" typical of the metaphysicals.

160 Brumm, Ursula. "Der 'Baum des Lebens' in der Meditationen Edward Taylors." *Jahrbuch für Amerikastudien*, XII (1967), 109-123.

English translation in No. 161. Takes issue with Halbert's interpretation of the tree of life image (No. 202), and shows how Taylor was a "theological" poet as opposed to the English metaphysicals who were "devotional" poets. Taylor's use of imagery resembles that of medieval artists; and because his "theological speculations led to such a splendor and sophistication of imagery," he was led "to conceal his meditations from his Puritan contemporaries and also from his descendants." (Cf. Hedberg, No. 203 and Werge, No. 278).

161 ———. "The 'Tree of Life' in Edward Taylor's Meditations." *Early American Literature*, III, No. 2 (1968), 72-87.

A translation of No. 160.

162 Burke, Herbert. [Review] *Library Journal*, LXXXIV (1959), 3778.

A favorable review of *The Poems* (Stanford, No. 3). "Existential vigor and religious subtlety ring in the poetry of Edward Taylor. . . ."

163 Bush, Sargent, Jr. "Paradox, Puritanism and Edward Taylor's *Gods Determinations*." *Early American Literature*, IV, No. 3 (1969–70), 48-66.

Resolves earlier disagreement between Warren (No. 273) and Pearce (No. 244) about whether or not Taylor's poetry is paradoxical. Discusses evidence in *Gods Determinations* which proves that Taylor consciously used paradox and that the Puritan world permitted it.

164 Callow, James T. "Edward Taylor Obeys St. Paul." *Early American Literature*, IV, No. 3 (1969–70), 89-96.

An explication of Meditations 1.19-22, which are based on St. Paul's "God hath highly exalted him." To understand the paradox in Taylor's wanting to write, yet feeling unworthy to write, it is necessary to go to the fuller context of the Biblical text, "that at the name of Jesus . . . every tongue should confess . . ." Taylor was obeying St. Paul in writing his Meditations.

165 Carlisle, E. F. "The Puritan Structure of Edward Taylor's Poetry." *American Quarterly*, XX (1968), 147-163.

Applies R. P. Blackmur's categories of "deep form" and "evident form" to show how "the underlying impulses and forms [of Taylor's *Meditations*] remain constant while the rhetorical strategies, logical patterns and methods of developing metaphor do change." Takes issue with Grabo (No. 4, pp. xxxiv-xliii) over the relationship between sermon and meditation; believes "the poem dramatizes the response of the *whole* Puritan man; whereas, the sermon develops the reasoning of the Puritan minister."

166 Chmaj, Betty E. "The Metaphors of Resurrection." *Universitas*, II (1964), 91-109.

Compares the use of metaphors from Isaiah, Revelations, and the Song of Songs in American-Finnish Lutheran hymns with their use by the American Puritans. Concludes the Finnish hymns lie "somewhere between Wigglesworth's gloom and Taylor's exuberance."

167 Clare, Sister M. Theresa. "Taylor's 'Meditation Sixty-Two.' " *Explicator*, XIX (1961), Item 16.

168 Clarke, J. A. [Review] *Library Journal*, LXXXVII (1962), 2904.

A favorable review of *Christographia* (Grabo, No. 4). The sermons have "a quaintness and charm" which will appeal even to those without theological interest.

169 Clendenning, John. "Piety and Imagery in Edward Taylor's 'The Reflexion.' " *American Quarterly*, XVI (1964), 203-210.

An interesting reversal of traditional typology is nevertheless "decidedly Puritan" in spirit. Instead of representing Christ as the bridegroom and the church or individual as his bride, in this poem Taylor represents himself as the bridegroom and Christ (symbolized by the Rose of Sharon) as the bride; Puritan piety "meant he had to pursue Christ" even though redemption for the Puritan was an "always unfulfilled quest."

170 ———. [Review] *Western Humanities Review*, XX (1966), 355-356. Reprinted in *Early American Literature Newsletter*, II, No. 1 (1967), 24.

A favorable review of the *Treatise Concerning the Lord's Supper* (Grabo, No. 8).

171 Coanda, Richard. [Review] *Renascence*, XV (1962), 96-97.

A review of *The Poems* (Stanford, No. 3).

172 Cochran, Robert W. [Review] *College English*, XXIV (1963), 489.

An unfavorable review of Grabo's *Edward Taylor* (No. 98). Feels Grabo is too scholarly in his treatment of Taylor criticism and too elementary in his discussion of mysticism.

173 Colacurcio, Michael J. "Gods Determinations Touching Half-Way Membership: Occasion and Audience in Edward Taylor." *American Literature*, XXXIX (1967), 298-314.

Gods Determinations speaks directly to the Half-Way Covenant controversy and displays a profound sense of audience which is not equalled again in American literature until Franklin. "The implied audience of the poem is precisely the half-way member of the Puritan congregation; the theme is the desirability of a more complete and active participation in a 'particular church' than that provided for by the Half-Way Covenant of 1662."

174 Curtis, Jared R. "Edward Taylor and Emily Dickinson: Voices and Visions." *Susquehana University Studies*, VII (1964), 159-167.

Edward Taylor is Emily Dickinson's spiritual ancestor and shares with her the doubleness of vision (inner and outer, finite and infinite) characteristic of the baroque. Both poets revel in "grotesque juxtapositions" of seemingly incongruous images, but Dickinson's "range of experience is not so wide or so rich" as Taylor's and her "keyboard of a single poem does not sound half the notes Taylor exuberantly plays at full organ."

175 Cutts, John P. [Review] *Books Abroad*, XXXV (1961), 345-346.

A generally favorable review of *The Poems* (Stanford, No. 3), but disagrees with Martz that Taylor's reputation must stand or fall on the *Preparatory Meditations*. Prefers the greater variety in *Gods Determinations*.

176 Damon, S. Foster. [Review] *The New England Quarterly*, XII (1939), 777-780.

A favorable review of *The Poetical Works* (Johnson, No. 1). "Not a great poet, Taylor was nevertheless a genuine one, who stands without apology with his spiritual kin, Anne Bradstreet and Michael Wigglesworth."

177 Davis, Thomas M. "Edward Taylor and the Traditions of Puritan Typology." *Early American Literature*, IV, No. 3 (1969–70), 27-47.

The sources of Taylor's typology are the Patristic and Protestant traditions, but these are modified (although always within the limits of Puritan Orthodoxy) when he feels the traditional interpretations are too confining. Uses typology in the *Treatise Concerning the Lord's Supper* to show that Stoddard was not just "drifting" away from the New England Way, but was refuting 200 years of Protestant theology; and the interpretations of the types become more personal as Taylor becomes more involved in the controversy. (For a fuller discussion see No. 286.)

178 Diebold, Robert K. [Review] *Carleton Miscellany*, VIII (1967), 127.

A favorable review of Stanford's *Edward Taylor* (No. 100).

179 Drake, Robert. "Felicitous Form." *Christian Century*, LXXVII (1960), 1060.

A favorable review of *The Poems* (Stanford, No. 3). Agrees with Martz that Taylor's reputation depends on the *Preparatory Meditations*.

180 Emerson, Everett H. [Review] *Seventeenth-Century News*, XXIV (1966), 65.

A favorable review of Stanford's *Edward Taylor* (No. 100), although he regrets that Stanford's approach did not leave him "much opportunity for criticism."

181 Fender, Stephen. "Edward Taylor and 'The Application of Redemption.'" *Modern Language Review*, LIX (1964), 331-334.

Disagrees with Martz (Nos. 113, 114) that the meditational system of St. Ignatius Loyola, known to the Puritans via Baxter, fully accounts for Taylor's meditations. Believes Thomas Hooker's *Application of Redemption* may have influenced him. "Certainly the juxtaposition of exalted and homely is extreme enough in Taylor to set him off from other 'poets of meditation'; it may well be that Hooker's influence provides a clue."

182 Gannett, Lewis. [Review] *New York Herald Tribune Books*, September 4, 1960, p. 6.

A favorable review of *The Poems* (Stanford, No. 3). Taylor is "America's finest Colonial poet."

183 Garrison, Joseph M., Jr. "Teaching Early American Literature: Some Suggestions." *College English*, XXXI (1970), 487-497.

Suggests ways of discussing dramatic situation in Taylor's poems in order to understand early American literature as literature and not merely as intellectual and cultural documents. Taylor is a poet "who discerns the theological presumptuousness of the first generation Puritans and tries to meet it openly and honestly in the anguished drama of his *Meditations*."

184 ———. "The 'Worship-Mould': A Note on Edward Taylor's *Preparatory Meditations*." *Early American Literature*, III, No. 2 (1968), 127-131.

Taylor's *Meditations* are "not eccentric imitations, but movements of faith cast in a 'Worship-mould.'" Taylor deliberately chose his stanza form to reinforce his theme. "Formal structure, in other words, would seem to affirm the poet's commitment and hope."

185 Garrison, W. E. "Puritan Treasure Trove." *Christian Century*, LVI (1939), 1508.

A generally favorable review of *The Poetical Works* (Johnson, No. 1). "Taylor's poetry is intensely religious and thoroughly Puritan, but he exhibits the more attractive side of the Puritan mind."

186 Giovannini, G. "Taylor's *The Glory of and Grace in the Church Set Out.*" *Explicator*, VI (1948), Item 26.

An answer to an inquiry in V (1947), Q-16, regarding the "Artificial angels."

187 Goodman, William B. "Edward Taylor Writes His Love." *New England Quarterly*, XXVII (1954), 510-515.

Newly transcribes Taylor's love letter to Elizabeth Fitch (see No. 10) and uses it to show that the metaphysical style was entirely natural to Taylor. "Taylor simply does not tail off a major school as, for example, John Cleveland does, but rather inhabits a realm where literature is not the first issue." Hence problems of literary influence are not important in understanding Taylor.

188 Grabo, Norman S. " 'The Appeale Tried': Another Edward Taylor Manuscript." *American Literature*, XXXIV (1962), 394-400.

A pamphlet from Taylor's "Manuscript Notebook," which had been falsely attributed to Stoddard in the Prince Library Catalogue, was really written by Taylor. "The Appeale Tried" is a strong rebuttal of Stoddard's *Appeal to the Learned* and a defense of the Mathers in the controversy over the Lord's Supper. It is important because "it belies Professor Miller's speculation [see No. 117] that Taylor was content to remain quietly on the frontier during the controversy" and because it "qualifies the impression Miller builds up so well of Stoddard's superior sense and reason in his attack on the Mathers. . . ."

189 ———. "Catholic Tradition, Puritan Literature, and Edward Taylor." *Papers of the Michigan Academy of Science, Arts and Letters*, XLV (1960), 395-402.

Accepts Stanford's demonstration of Taylor's orthodoxy as a Puritan Calvinist (No. 260), and from there goes on to discuss "the question of Taylor's inherent Catholicism, not to deny it, because it is there, but to suggest that it is thoroughly possible to create a Puritan literature within a Catholic tradition, that Puritans in both old and New England knew that it was possible, and that Edward Taylor knowingly undertook the task."

190 ———. "Edward Taylor on the Lord's Supper." *Boston Public Library Quarterly*, XII (1960), 22-36.

An important discussion of Taylor's controversy with Stoddard over the Lord's Supper. Summarizes and analyzes the major documents, including Taylor's ordination-day sermon "A Particular Church is God's House" (see Nos. 36, 42). Shows that Taylor was a federal theologian as well as an orthodox Calvinist.

191 ———. "Edward Taylor's Spiritual Huswifery." *Publications of the Modern Language Association*, LXXIX (1964), 554-560.

Traces the huswifery image through Taylor's poetry and shows how it progressively represents love in friendship, the English language, love in the union of husband and wife, and ultimately (in "Huswifery" itself) the "Holy robes for glory" or the "wedden garment" in the soul's union with Christ. The poem "Huswifery," then, is really a preparatory meditation for the union with Christ in the Lord's Supper.

191a ———. "*Gods Determinations*: Touching Taylor's Critics." *Seventeenth-Century News*, XXVIII (1970), 22-24.

An important discussion of the past, present, and future of Taylor criticism. While critics of the *Preparatory Meditations* have moved from problems of definition to problems of evaluation, critics of *Gods Determinations* have not yet passed beyond the definition stage. The few critics who have devoted attention to *Gods Determinations* in the 1960s are still trying to say "what the poem is instead of how it is."

Disagrees with Martz' opinion that *Gods Determinations* is merely "a labor of versified doctrine." Believes that it will ultimately prove to be "the fixed star in Taylor's critical firmament," and that until it receives more sensitive criticism, "the best current criticism must be considered essentially tentative and preliminary."

192 ———. "The Poet to the Pope: Edward Taylor to Solomon Stoddard." *American Literature*, XXXII (1960), 197-201.

A discussion of Taylor's controversy with Stoddard and of the sermons in which Taylor defends the orthodox view of the Lord's Supper. Includes a transcription of Taylor's and Stoddard's letters from Taylor's manuscript "Commonplace Book" (No. 18).

193 ———. [Review] *American Literature*, XLI (1969), 116-117.

A generally favorable review of Nicolaisen's *Die Bildlichkeit in der Dichtung Edward Taylors* (No. 99), although Grabo regrets there is no discussion of single poems to demonstrate the application of his principles in depth. Feels he persuasively argues the relationship between Taylor's imagery and the mystical tradition.

194 ———. [Review] *Seventeenth-Century News*, XXIV (1966), 64-65.

A review of the 1966 edition of *The Poetical Works* (Johnson, No. 9). The edition is now of value mainly for historical reasons. Only slight revision of the 1939 edition, with a Bibliographical Postscript which is "quite inadequate and partially inaccurate." The critical apparatus has been "superseded or incorporated into easily accessible form elsewhere," but the description of Taylor's library is invaluable.

195 ———. [Review] *William and Mary Quarterly*, Series 3, XVIII (1961), 140-142.

A generally favorable review of *The Poems* (Stanford, No. 3). Admires Martz's analysis of the meditative tradition (in Nos. 113, 114).

196 ———. "Taylor's 'Sacramental Meditation Six.'" *Explicator*, XVIII (1960), Item 40.

In contrast to McNamara (No. 231), Grabo sees no reason why the imagery of the meditation should correspond with the scriptural epigraph; both illustrate the sermon doctrine, which was chosen first.

197 ———. "The Veiled Vision: The Role of Aesthetics in Early American Intellectual History." *William and Mary Quarterly*, XIX (1962), 493-510.

The most accurate picture of Puritan aesthetics is not to be found in Puritan statements about literature (which often recommend a "plain style") but in the literature itself, especially in the poetry. Mystical elements are far more common among Puritans than intellectual historians have realized, as both Taylor and Cotton Mather show. "Taylor certifies Mather's reeling and staggering and so adds a dimension to that debate for which Miller [see Nos. 117, 119] cannot account and which might need no accounting for were it not for its pervasiveness in the New England temperament, part of the shape of human feeling in the seventeenth century. This is what Taylor's poetry makes so clear."

198 [Grant, Douglas]. "Poet in a Wilderness." *Times Literary Supplement*, LX (1961), 72.

Reprinted in No. 107.

A not-very-favorable review of *The Poems* (Stanford, No. 3). Compares Taylor to Herbert, and concludes Taylor is not really meditative because after reading a few poems the rest can be predicted. "Taylor's imagination is utterly trapped in the Bible, and nothing exists unless it can have a Biblical phrase attached to it."

See replies in Letters column of succeeding issues: George Proctor and "Mr. Reviewer," p. 105; Jack Lindsay, p. 137; D. E. Stanford, p. 185.

199 Griffin, Edward M. "The Structure and Language of Taylor's Meditation 2.112." *Early American Literature*, III, No. 3 (1968–69), 205-208.

The logical conclusion of Meditation 2.112, based on the text "If one died for all then all are Dead," is that death is not to be feared by the elect. But the language and images of the Meditation seem to belie this assurance. Like many of the Meditations, this one therefore suffers from Taylor's "rigorous adherence to doctrine," and "the non-Calvinist can enter the world of his poetry only by a conscious suspension of disbelief."

200 Griffith, Clark. "Edward Taylor and the Momentum of Metaphor." *English Literary History*, XXXIII (1966), 448-460.

Two kinds of imagery cause an ascending movement in Taylor's poetry: allegory, in which the poet-penitent is concerned with revealing God; and conceit, in which the poet-creator is mainly occupied with the beauties of the language.

201 H. B. H. [Review] *Springfield Republican*, July 24, 1960, p. 4D.

A favorable review of *The Poems* (Stanford, No. 3).

202 Halbert, Cecelia L. "Tree of Life Imagery in the Poetry of Edward Taylor." *American Literature*, XXXVIII (1966), 22-34.

Taylor's Tree of Life imagery is based on its meaning in Genesis and Revelation, yet because he extends it beyond the Biblical meaning in a metaphysical manner, "we must regard him primarily as a poet working to sustain a metaphor, and only secondarily as a peculiarly Puritan poet of the seventeenth century." Relates Taylor to Herbert and Quarles and suggests direct influence by Marvell. (Cf. Brumm, No. 160; Hedberg, No. 203; and Werge, No. 278.)

203 Hedberg, Johannes. "Meditations Linguistic and Literary on 'Meditation Twenty-Nine' by Edward Taylor." *Moderna Språk* [Stockholm], LIV (1960), 253-270.

A controversial linguistic and thematic explication of the Tree of Life image in the poem. (Cf. Brumm, No. 160; Halbert, No. 202; and Werge, No. 278.)

204 ———. [Review] *Moderna Språk* [Stockholm], LVI (1962), 422-425.

A review of *The Poems* (Stanford, No. 3).

205 Hodges, Robert R. "Edward Taylor's 'Artificiall Man.' " *American Literature*, XXXI (1959), 76-77.

Explains the obscure allusion to the "Artifical man Aquinas slew" in Meditation 2.56 as a reference to the artificial human head which, according to legend, Aquinas' teacher Albertus Magnus had made and Aquinas had destroyed.

206 Hughes, Daniel. "Helping People Live Their Lives." *Voices*, CLXXIV (1961), 54-56.

A generally favorable review of *The Poems* (Stanford, No. 3).

207 Hutchison, Percy. "Edward Taylor: Early American Poet of Mysticism." *New York Times Book Review*, January 28, 1940, p. 3.

A brief, favorable review of *The Poetical Works* (Johnson, No. 1).

208 Israel, Calvin. "Edward Taylor's *Barleybreaks.*" *American Notes and Queries*, IV (1966), 147-148.

An explication of Meditation 1.40.

209 Jacobs, Hayes B. "Stop Picking on Edward Taylor!" *Harper's Magazine*, May 1960, pp. 71-72.

A humorous, sympathetic essay meant to "enlist support for my Save Taylor project," i.e., save Taylor from the critics.

210 Johnson, Thomas H. "Colonial Voice Reheard in Verse." *Saturday Review*, August 6, 1960, p. 24.

A review of *The Poems* (Stanford, No. 3). Acknowledges this text to be the definitive edition of Taylor's poetry. "But, in my opinion, in its effort to focus attention on the 128 'Meditations' here published for the first time, it unwarrantably downgrades 'Gods Determinations.' "

211 ———. "The Discovery of Edward Taylor's Poetry." In Adams, No. 137, pp. 101-104.

212 ———. "A Seventeenth-Century Printing of Some Verses of Edward Taylor." *New England Quarterly*, XIV (1941), 139-141.

Reprints and discusses Taylor's condolence letter to Samuel Sewell containing Stanzas 5 and 7 of "Upon Wedlock and Death of Children," which had been printed following the last page of Cotton Mather's *Right Thoughts in Sad Hours* (Nos. 17, 19).

213 Johnston, Thomas E., Jr. "Edward Taylor: An American Emblematist." *Early American Literature*, III, No. 3 (1968–69), 186-198.

Adapted from his doctoral dissertation (No. 294). Shows how Taylor "modified a centuries old tradition in particularly Puritanical ways." As emblematist, Taylor consciously sees himself as poet or "maker" of emblems, and consciously desires God to make Taylor his emblem ("Make me, O Lord . . .").

214 ———. "A Note on the Voices of Anne Bradstreet, Edward Taylor, Roger Williams, and Philip Pain." *Early American Literature*, III, No. 2 (1968), 125-126.

Disagrees with Murdock (No. 122) that Mather's phrase "a little recreation of poetry" adequately describes the Puritan attitude toward poetry. It is necessary to look at the poets themselves to discover their attitudes toward poetry. (For a more extensive discussion by Johnston on this subject see No. 294).

215 Jones, Howard M. "Discovery: Unexpected Find of Forgotten Poet." *Boston Evening Transcript*, December 30, 1939, p. 5.

A noncommittal review of *The Poetical Works* (Johnson, No. 1). Taylor "could not avoid the conceits which mar much of the poetry of his century."

216 Jordan, Raymond J. "Taylor's 'The Ebb and Flow.' " *Explicator*, XX (1962), Item 67.

The images of tinder and censer metaphorically represent the ebb and flow of Taylor's confidence in his election.

217 Jorgenson, Chester E. [Review] *Criticism*, IV (1962), 271.

A favorable review of *The Poems* (Stanford, No. 3), especially of Stanford's critical apparatus. Feels Taylor was an important religious-meditative poet, if not one of the best.

218 Junkins, Donald. "Edward Taylor's Creative Process." *Early American Literature*, IV, No. 3 (1969–70), 67-78.

Resolves disagreement between Grabo (No. 4, pp. xxxiv-xliii) and Benton (No. 154) regarding the relationship between sermons and meditations. The meditational poem is based on the doctrine of the sermon, for which the text is only a point of departure. Hence "Taylor's creative process is only understandable in the context of his mystic Puritanism," and is at once a religious and aesthetic experience.

219 ———. "Edward Taylor's Revisions." *American Literature*, XXXVII (1965), 135-152.

An important article which challenges critics to consider the technical and aesthetic aspects of Taylor's verse. Points out that so far three critics had accused him of being a negligent craftsman, either because as a Puritan he was more concerned with message than technique (Lind, No. 228 and Pearce, No. 244) or because he did not polish his poems for publication (Blau, No. 157); but no critics to date had challenged these opinions. Examines early versions of some of the Meditations which were found stuffed in the binding of the manuscript "Poetical Works"

(No. 50), and concludes that Taylor was a conscious craftsman whose roughness was often deliberate: "in many places the very fiber of the poem depends upon this roughness and Taylor was not only aware of it; he consciously strove to achieve it."

220 ———. " 'Should Stars Wooe Lobster Claws?': A Study of Edward Taylor's Poetic Practice and Theory." *Early American Literature*, III, No. 2 (1968), 88-117.

Discusses Taylor's compulsion to write in spite of his inadequacies, and his consequent anguish. Criticism of Taylor to date has not perceived the organic unity in his religious-aesthetic experience, and has led people like Miller to talk about his didacticism (Nos. 117, 118). "What has been mistaken for didacticism is in reality the exploratory mystic-religious consciousness at work. Taylor's art was his religion and his religion was his life." (For a fuller discussion see No. 295.)

221 Kaiser, Leo M. and Donald E. Stanford. "The Latin Poems of 'Edward Taylor.' " *Yale University Library Gazette,* XL (1965), 75-81.

Prints two Latin elegies (with English translations by Kaiser) from the manuscript "Poetical Works" which had been mistakenly attributed to Taylor on the death of Chauncy. Actually they are by Chauncy on the death of John Davenport.

222 Keller, Karl. "The Example of Edward Taylor." *Early American Literature*, IV, No. 3 (1969–70), 5-26.

Taylor's attitude toward poetry explains both his injunction against publication, and what is peculiarly American about him. The process of writing is more important to Taylor than the finished product; that process was one of meditation and self-discovery. Hence the poems were meant to be private—a typically American attitude.

223 ———. "The Rev. Mr. Edward Taylor's Bawdry." *New England Quarterly*, XLIII (1970), 382-406.

Analyzes Taylor's use of scatological imagery (emblematic of man's sinful state) and erotic imagery (symbolic of the salvation of the elect). Shows that Taylor's use of this imagery (contrary to the opinion of earlier critics) is neither unorthodox nor peculiar to Puritanism. Rather, the contrast between scatalogical and erotic symbolizes the tensions inherent in the Christian drama of salvation.

224 ———. " 'The World Slickt up in Types': Edward Taylor as a Version of Emerson." *Early American Literature*, V, No. 1 (1970), 124-140.

Because Taylor does not take types as seriously as other Puritans, but plays with them wittily until they are personally relevant, and because nature and the created world are of more importance for him, his poetry foreshadows that of the transcendentalists. Just as nature for Emerson attains meaning by its correspondence with the over-soul, likewise for Taylor nature, or types, are meaningful only because of the anti-types. (See also Davis, Nos. 177, 286. Cf. Lowance, No. 296.)

225 Lang, Erdmute. " 'Meditation 42' von Edward Taylor." *Jahrbuch für Amerikastudien*, XII (1967), 92-108.

Discusses Taylor in the meditative tradition and shows that theology and personal creed are more important for him than literary form. Each Meditation and each stanza has a similar tripartite division according to the traditional faculties—memory, understanding, and will.

226 Laurentia, Sister M. "Taylor's *Meditation 42*." *Explicator*, VIII (1949), Item 19.

227 Levy, B. M. [Review] *William and Mary Quarterly*, Series 3, XX (1963), 291-293.

A favorable review of *Christographia* (Grabo, No. 4).

228 Lind, Sidney E. "Edward Taylor: A Revaluation." *New England Quarterly*, XXI (1948), 518-530.

Taylor has had too much critical attention paid him: "he is at best a mediocre poet, as he was doomed to be, by his station in life."

229 Manierre, William R., II. "Verbal Patterns in the Poetry of Edward Taylor." *College English*, XXIII (1962), 296-299.

A rhetorical analysis of Taylor's use of some classical devices like ploce and polypton. His verbal wit is not merely ornamental, but has a structural function and is characteristic of the seventeenth-century "word-centered" as opposed to "thing-centered" epistemology.

230 Martin, L. C. [Review] *Modern Language Review*, LVI (1961), 590-591.

A generally favorable review of *The Poems* (Stanford, No. 3).

230a McGiffert, Michael. "American Puritan Studies in the 1960s." *William and Mary Quarterly*, XXVII (1970), 36-67.

A discussion of recent critical reappraisals of older attitudes toward Puritan aesthetics, especially those of Perry Miller. The concern of scholars with mysticism and typology in Taylor's poetry is characteristic of the new critical approaches.

231 McNamara, Anne Marie. "Taylor's 'Sacramental Meditation Six.' " *Explicator*, XVII (1958), Item 3.

Relates the epigram "I am the lilley of the valleys" to the coin imagery of the poem; both symbolize purity, and Taylor's yoking them in one poem shows his intuitive perception and his metaphysical mode. (See Grabo's answer in No. 196.)

232 Meserole, Harrison T. [Review] *Seventeenth-Century News*, XIX (1961), 25.

A favorable review of *The Poems* (Stanford, No. 3). Praises Stanford's meticulous editing and Martz' illuminating introduction.

233 Mignon, Charles W. "Another Taylor Manuscript at Yale." *Yale University Library Gazette*, XLI (1966), 72-73

Describes Taylor's "Manuscript Notebook" (No. 47).

234 ———. "Diction in Edward Taylor's *Preparatory Meditations.*" *American Speech*, XXXXI (1966), 243-253.

A study of dialect words, obsolete words, and medical-scientific terms in Taylor's poetry shows that his diction is "dangerously obscure in contrast to his orthodoxly comprehensible contemporaries." This obscurity is explained, however, by the private purpose of Taylor's *Meditations*.

235 ———. "Edward Taylor's *Preparatory Meditations*: A Decorum of Imperfection." *Publications of the Modern Language Association*, LXXXIII (1968), 1423-1428.

As a Puritan, Taylor believed that man is totally depraved and cannot write poetry at all without grace. Therefore his poetry must be judged according to a "decorum of imperfection" which is distinct from the metaphysical decorum.

236 ———. "A Principle of Order in Edward Taylor's *Preparatory Meditations.*" *Early American Literature*, IV, No. 3 (1969–70), 110-116.

Uses Meditation 2.43 to show that the three-fold order in each meditation (Examination—Meditation on doctrine—Application of doctrine) is responsible for the feeling of sameness about the *Meditations*. A kind of frozen tension or stasis results from the contrast between earthly doubt and heavenly certitude.

237 ———. "Some Notes on the History of the Edward Taylor Manuscripts." *Yale University Library Gazette*, XXXIX (1965), 168-173.

A general summary of the facts known to date about the Taylor manuscripts. Includes a transcription of Ezra Stiles' "Memoir" of Taylor (No. 90).

238 Miller, Perry. "A 'Revolutionary Discovery' in Poetry." *Christian Science Monitor*, June 23, 1960, p. 9.

A review of *The Poems* (Stanford, No. 3) which is favorable concerning the editing of the text. Feels Martz's Foreword is "the wisest estimate of Taylor that has yet appeared," but "Mr. Stanford regrettably supplies to this edition a crude attempt to expound Taylor's 'theology.' "

239 Monteiro, George. "Taylor's 'Meditation 8.' " *Explicator*, xxvii (1969), Item 45.

240 Morris, W. S. [Review] *Church History*, xxxvi (1967), 226-227.

A favorable review of the *Treatise Concerning the Lord's Supper* (Grabo, No. 8).

241 Murphy, Francis. "An Edward Taylor Manuscript Book." *American Literature*, xxxi (1959), 188-189.

Mentions the discovery in the Westfield Athenaeum of a second manuscript given by Oliver Brewster Taylor—a transcription in English of two works of Origen of Alexandria: *Contra Celsus* and *De Principiis* (No. 41).

242 ———. "Edward Taylor's Attitude Toward Publication: A Question Concerning Authority." *American Literature*, xxxiv (1962) 393-394.

The idea that Taylor forbade his heirs to publish is based only on family tradition as recorded in Sprague, No. 90 and Sibley, No. 85. While some critics have referred to Taylor's will as the origin of the supposed injunction, there is no evidence of such a will. The Probate Office of Hampshire County, Massachusetts records that he died intestate. (See No. 66.)

243 ———. [Review] *New England Quarterly*, xl (1967), 153-155.

A favorable review of the *Treatise Concerning the Lord's Supper* (Grabo, No. 8). The sermons, "a remarkable description of Puritan piety," deserve more critical attention. Commends Grabo's editing.

244 Pearce, Roy Harvey. "Edward Taylor: The Poet as Puritan." *New England Quarterly*, xxiii (1950), 31-46.

Reprinted in No. 125. While Taylor is the best of the colonial poets, he is not a great poet, and we have neglected to read him in the context of his Puritanism. His poetry is not so much concerned with human experience as with showing the nature of the divine order in the world; consequently it lacks paradox and drama. The Puritan attitude that art is only a means to an end made Taylor a weak technician.

245 Penner, Allen R. "Edward Taylor's Meditation One." *American Literature*, XXXIX (1967), 193-199.

It is necessary to understand Taylor's theology as expressed in *Christographia* in order to appreciate the *Meditations*. Meditation One, like the others, is "an acknowledgement of man's spiritual inadequacy and his utter dependence upon the grace of God."

246 Pérez Gallego, Cándido. " 'Sweet' en Edward Taylor." *Filologia Moderna*, VI (1966), 273-292.

247 Plumstead, Arthur W. "Puritanism and Nineteenth-Century American Literature." *Queen's Quarterly*, LXX (1963), 209-227.

Discusses the importance of the New England Puritans to an understanding of the American literary tradition, especially in regard to the American Dream, nineteenth-century symbolism, and the conflicts between reason and emotion, individual and society.

247a Pochman, Henry A. [Review] *Early American Literature*, III, No. 2 (Fall, 1968), 134-135.

A neutral review of Nicolaisen's *Die Bildlichkeit in der Dichtung Edward Taylors* (No. 99). Feels that Nicholaisen over-emphasizes the Biblical sources of Taylor's images and provides too little documentation.

248 Prosser, Evan. "Edward Taylor's Poetry." *New England Quarterly*, XXXX (1967), 375-398.

Taylor's use of scripture as a basis for his poems indicates that he "is not engaged in independent inquiry so much as in contemplation of an already revealed truth." His poetry is limited by his Puritan framework and exists in a closed world in which all tensions are resolved and "in which God, Nature and man are in blessed harmony."

249 Reiter, Robert. "Poetry and Typology: Edward Taylor's *Preparatory Meditations*, Second Series, Numbers 1-30." *Early American Literature*, V, No. 1 (1970), 111-123.

Discusses these thirty meditations as a series on typological subjects, probably related to corresponding sermons. The meditations on personal types of Christ are better than those on rituals. Occasionally Taylor combines type, meditation and personal application into a successful poem on a difficult, "unpoetic" subject.

250 Rowe, Karen. "A Biblical Illumination of Taylorian Art." *American Literature*, XL (1968), 370-374.

Shows that the text of Meditation 2.27 is not Exodus 29:20 as Stanford had said (No. 30), but Leviticus 13:45–46 and 14: 1–32, a much more illuminating text for the poem as a whole.

251 Russell, Gene. "Taylor's 'Upon Wedlock, and Death of Children.' " *Explicator*, XXVII (1969), Item 71.

252 Scheick, William J. "A Viper's Nest, The Featherbed of Faith: Edward Taylor on the Will." *Early American Literature*, V (1970), 45-56.

A discussion of the respective roles of reason and will in Taylor's poetry; "the will or heart—Taylor used the terms interchangeably—is the central faculty engaged in the drama of conversion."

253 Schultz, Fritz W. [Review] *Archiv für das Studium der neueren Sprachen und Literaturen*, CII (1965), 140-143.

A review of *The Poems* (Stanford, No. 3).

254 Secor, Robert. "Taylor's 'Upon a Spider Catching A Fly.' " *Explicator*, XXVI (1968), Item 42.

Argues that Stanford (No. 100, p. 36) oversimplifies the poem by allegorizing it. The first six stanzas are "less an allegory of man and Satan than an illustration from nature," and thus the poem "teaches by example not allegory."

255 Shepherd, Emmy. "Edward Taylor's Injunction Against Publication." *American Literature*, XXXIII (1962), 512-513.

None of the previous explanations of why Taylor forbade his heirs to publish is satisfactory, since Miller (No. 119) and Murdock (No. 122) have shown the Puritans were not averse to poetry, and since Grabo (No. 98) and Stanford (No. 260) have established his orthodoxy. The only reasonable explanation is "simple, genuine humility, touched by self-respect and pride in his work and perhaps—lightly—by the perversity of the aged."

256 Siebel, Kathy and Thomas M. Davis. "Edward Taylor and the Cleansing of *Aqua Vitae*." *Early American Literature*, IV, No. 3 (1969–70), 102-109.

A discussion of the use of aqua vitae as a metaphor for Christ's saving Grace in Meditations 1.10, 32; 2.4, 60B, 75, and 111.

257 Smith, A. J. [Review.] *Review of English Studies*, New Series, XIII (1962), 80-82.

An unfavorable review of *The Poems* (Stanford, No. 3). Taylor is a "curious survival" of the metaphysical poets and "an incorrigible flaunter of obsolete fashion."

258 ———. [Review] *Review of English Studies*, New Series, XV (1964), 434-435.

An unfavorable review of *Christographia* (No. 4) in regard to the text, but favorable in regard to the editing. Taylor is "an academic preacher of uncompromising rigour."

259 Smith, Carleton S. [Review] *New England Quarterly*, XXXVI (1963), 559-564.

A generally favorable review of Grabo's *Edward Taylor* (No. 98) and his edition of *Christographia* (No. 4). Prefers Taylor's poems to his sermons because they are "much less stilted and more appealing."

260 Stanford, Donald E. "Edward Taylor and the Lord's Supper." *American Literature*, XXVII (1955), 172-178.

An important essay which settles the debate over Taylor's orthodoxy. Stanford shows that where Murdock (No. 122) and Weathers (No. 275) had considered Taylor unorthodox and where Johnson (No. 1) had considered him orthodox in the context of covenant or federal theology, Taylor is actually an orthodox Calvinist. His Meditations rejecting Stoddardeanism, a close examination of Calvin, and "mystical" qualities in other Puritan divines like Cotton Mather all provide evidence that both as preacher and as poet Taylor was entirely orthodox in his attitude toward the Lord's Supper.

261 ———. "Edward Taylor's Metrical History of Christianity." *American Literature*, XXXIII (1961), 279-297.

Discusses the long narrative poem still in manuscript at the time of the article (see No. 5) and discusses some of the shortcomings and virtues of seventeenth- and early eighteenth-century New England Calvinism which it points up. "Taylor, like most New England Puritans, was lacking in literary taste. The poet who could write great religious meditative verse could also write the most deadly doggerel."

262 ———. "[Letter] To The Editor." *Early American Literature*, V, No. 2 (1970), 60-61.

Clarifies an error in an earlier article by Thomas Davis (No. 177) in which Davis had ascribed to Stanford a theory which is really Norman Grabo's.

263 ———. [Review] *American Literature*, XXXIV (1962), 412.

A review of Grabo's *Edward Taylor* (No. 98). Finds it a useful introduction to Taylor, especially good on the Stoddard controversy; but feels it exaggerates the mystical aspects of Taylor's poetry.

264 ———. [Review] *American Literature*, XXXV (1963), 242-243.

A generally favorable review of *Christographia* (Grabo, No. 4). Commends Grabo's editing.

265 ———. [Review] *American Literature*, XXXIX (1967), 112.

A favorable review of the *Treatise Concerning the Lord's Supper* (Grabo, No. 8).

266 Streeter, Robert E. [Review] *College English*, XXIII (1962), 690.

A favorable review of *The Poems* (Stanford, No. 3).

267 Tedeschini Lalli, Biancamaria. "Edward Taylor." *Studi Americani*, No. 2 (1956), pp. 9-43.

268 Thomas, Jean L. "Drama and Doctrine in *Gods Determinations*." *American Literature*, XXXVI (1965), 452-462.

Finds in the medieval homiletic tradition a more likely source for *Gods Determinations* than the morality-play tradition (see Wright, No. 282). But Taylor's account of "man's spiritual pilgrimage lacks one element vital to the medieval view of salvation: the theme of 'The Fool Grown Wise.'. . . It is unfortunate, I think, that Taylor has not sufficiently developed the relationship between Christian doctrine and the human condition of Puritan man."

269 Thorpe, Peter. "Edward Taylor as Poet." *New England Quarterly*, XXXIX (1966), 356-372.

Extends Junkins' argument (No. 219) that Taylor is a deliberate and skilled craftsman and often revised his poems. Argues that irregularities in imagery, diction, punctation, syntax, and metrics are often functional.

270 Van Doren, Mark. "Poetry Long in Waiting." *New York Herald Tribune Books*, October 29, 1939, p. 24.

A generally favorable review of *The Poetical Works* (Johnson, No. 1). Unlike Johnson, Van Doren feels Taylor does his best when he does not develop one single figure: "The mechanics of the 'conceit' overwhelmed him too often, landing him in monotony."

271 Wallace, Robert. [Review] *New England Quarterly*, XXXIII (1960), 542-544.

A generally favorable review of *The Poems* (Stanford, No. 3).

272 Walsh, James P. "Solomon Stoddard's Open Communion: A Re-examination." *New England Quarterly*, XLIII (1970), 97-114.

Brief mention of Taylor's role in the Stoddardean controversy. Challenges Perry Miller's interpretation that open communion was "an attempt to frustrate the democratic forces of the frontier by turning those forces against themselves." Rather, Stoddard was careful to insist that the sacrament could be a "converting ordinance" only to the visible saints, and did not want voluntary church membership.

273 Warren, Austin. "Edward Taylor's Poetry: Colonial Baroque." *Kenyon Review*, III (1941), 355-371.

Revised and reprinted in No. 135. An important early article —the first after Johnson to give extended attention to Taylor's poetic abilities. Argues that "baroque" is a better description of Taylor's poetry than "metaphysical" (cf. Brown, No. 159). The *Meditations* display a sacramental conception of the world which was "not absent from—but only restricted by—Puritanism and Nonconformity." Hence Taylor was something of an anomaly among Puritan poets. Prefers the *Meditations* to *Gods Determinations*.

274 ———. "Meditations of a Poet." *New York Times Book Review*, July 24, 1960, pp. 5, 18.

A favorable review of *The Poems* (Stanford, No. 3).

275 Weathers, Willie T. "Edward Taylor and the Cambridge Platonists." *American Literature*, XXVI (1954), 1-31.

The influence of the Cambridge Platonists on Taylor explains the many pagan-Christian parallels in his imagery, and how he could be both "a good New England Puritan and so good a poet." *Gods Determinations* is not really about the elect in Calvinist terms, but a drama of universal salvation.

276 ———. "Edward Taylor, Hellenistic Puritan." *American Literature*, XVIII (1946), 18-26.

Disagrees with Wright (No. 282) about Taylor's lack of classical background. Discusses the Greek and Roman poets in Taylor's library and finds classical influence in several poems. Taylor's classicism accounts for his injunction not to publish.

277 Weber, Alfred. "Edward Taylor: Besprechung einer Taylor-Ausgabe und Notizen zu einem Forschungsbericht." *Jahrbuch für Amerikastudien*, VII (1962), 320-334.

A review of *The Poems* (Stanford, No. 3), and discussion of Taylor's poetry.

278 Werge, Thomas. "The Tree of Life in Edward Taylor's Poetry: The Sources of a Puritan Image." *Early American Literature, III*, No. 3 (1968–69), 199-204.

Discusses the theological sources of the image, in contrast to Carlisle (No. 165) and Halbert (No. 202), who have insisted on its aesthetic, literary sources. Shows how Augustine's concept of "seminal nature" and the whole theological-metaphorical tradition is more important than, for example, specific images of tree and garden which Halbert emphasizes in Marvell and Quarles.

279 Williams, Stanley T. [Review] In Adams (No. 137), 101.

A favorable review of *The Poetical Works* (Johnson, No. 1). Describes Taylor as the "frontier parson . . . quietly writing verse in the service of God," who forbade publication because the "passionate impulse within him to create beauty" was inconsistent with his Puritanism.

280 Winslow, Ola E. [Review] *William and Mary Quarterly*, Series 3, XIX (1962), 611-612.

A favorable review of Grabo's *Edward Taylor* (No. 98). Finds it a major contribution in revealing an aspect of Puritanism not well understood—the devotional and mystical.

281 Woodward, Robert H. "Automata in Hawthorne's 'Artist of the Beautiful' and Taylor's 'Meditation 56.' " *Emerson Society Quarterly*, No. 31 (1963), pp. 63-66.

Discusses the way in which both Taylor and Hawthorne use examples of traditional mechanical "marvels" like the artifical human head of Albertus Magnus.

282 Wright, Nathalia. "The Morality Tradition in the Poetry of Edward Taylor." *American Literature*, XVIII (1946), 1-17.

Emphasizes the dramatic element in Taylor's poetry, most obvious in *Gods Determinations*. First critic after Johnson (No. 20) to agree that *Gods Determinations* is Taylor's best. Shows the influence of the morality play tradition and the lack of influence from classical literature. (Cf. Weathers, No. 276.)

K. Dissertations and Theses

283 Becker, Arnold. "Edward Taylor's Looking Glass: A Chapter in the History of an Image." Unpublished M. A. thesis, Pennsylvania State University, 1963.

284 Berkowitz, Morton. "Edward Taylor and the Seventeenth Century." Unpublished thesis, University of Massachusetts, 1968.

285 Cooper, Sister M. Scholastica. "A Study of the American Puritan Poet Edward Taylor in Relation to Seventeenth-Century English Poetry." Unpublished M. A. thesis, University of Minnesota, 1956.

286 Davis, Thomas M. "The Traditions of Puritan Typology." Unpublished doctoral dissertation, University of Missouri, 1968. *Dissertation Abstracts,* XXIX (1969), 3094A.

Traces the tradition of typology from the early Christian fathers to the seventeenth century, then analyzes Edward Taylor and Jonathan Edwards, both theologically and artistically, as a part of that tradition. Of all the Puritans, Taylor was the most knowledgeable about and most influenced by the tradition. (See No. 177.)

287 Dunn, Hough-Lewis. "Edward Taylor's Poetic Sequences." Unpublished dissertation, University of Texas, 1966.

288 Epperson, William Russell. "The Meditative Structure of Edward Taylor's 'Preparatory Meditations.' " Unpublished doctoral dissertation, University of Kansas, 1965. *Dissertation Abstracts*, XXVII (1966), 770A.

Outlines the traditional meditational method, surveys the Puritan understanding of it, and shows how the *Preparatory Meditations* are structured on it.

289 Fender, Stephen. "Edward Taylor and the Sources of American Puritan Wit." Unpublished dissertation, Manchester University [England], 1962–63.

290 Gilman, Harvey. "From Sin to Song: Image Clusters and Patterns in Edward Taylor's *Preparatory Meditations*." Unpublished doctoral dissertation, Pennsylvania State University, 1967. *Dissertation Abstracts*, XXVIII (1968), 4126A.

A close reading of the 217 Meditations reveals "significant stylistic and technical development," which in turn reflects changes in Taylor's "situation"; stylistic variety within the threefold meditational structure; and a pattern of thought and images which moves from sin to song, both in each individual meditation, and in the sequence as a whole.

291 Grabo, Norman S. "Edward Taylor's *Christographia* Sermons: A Study of Their Relationship to His *Sacramental Meditations*, with an Edition of the Sermons." Unpublished doctoral dissertation, University of California at Los Angeles, 1958.

The basis for Grabo's published edition of *Christographia* (No. 4).

292 Grose, Christopher. "To the American Strand: A Study of the Poetry of George Herbert and Edward Taylor." Unpublished B. A. Honors thesis, Amherst, 1961.

293 Howard, John. "An Analysis of the Poetic Technique of Edward Taylor's *Preparatory Meditations*." Unpublished M. A. thesis, University of Maryland, 1963.

294 Johnston, Thomas E., Jr. "American Puritan Poetic Voices: Essays on Anne Bradstreet, Edward Taylor, Roger Williams, and Philip Pain." Unpublished doctoral dissertation, Ohio University, 1968. *Dissertation Abstracts,* XXIX (1969), 3141-3142A.

Four essays, including "Edward Taylor: An American Emblematist." Partially reprinted in Johnston, No. 213 (see also No. 214). In general "the Puritanesque voice, especially Taylor's, is an emblematic voice."

295 Junkins, Donald Arthur. "An Analytical Study of Edward Taylor's *Preparatory Meditations*." Unpublished doctoral dissertation, Boston University, 1963. *Dissertation Abstracts*, XXIV (1963), 2013-2014.

Taylor's orthodoxy is substantiated by a study of his poetic theory, his revisions, his mystical images, and the relationship between the fourteen *Christographia* sermons and corresponding Meditations. His orthodox Puritanism, which is "mystical as well as theological," demonstrates "the unified nature of Taylor's religious and aesthetic life as a testimony of his Puritanism." (See Nos. 218, 220.)

296 Lowance, Mason I., Jr. "Images and Shadows of Divine Things: Puritan Typology in New England from 1660 to 1750." Unpublished doctoral dissertation, Emory University, 1967. *Dissertation Abstracts*, XXVIII (1968), 4255-4256A.

A study of Puritan typology in works of John Cotton, Samuel Mather, Edward Taylor, and Jonathan Edwards. Mather and Taylor did not follow the liberalizing of typological interpretations based on nature, but kept to Biblical sources, as Edwards and Emerson did not. (Cf. Davis, Nos. 177, 286 and Keller, No. 224.)

297 Mignon, Charles W., Jr. "The American Puritan and Private Qualities of Edward Taylor, the Poet." Unpublished doctoral dissertation, University of Connecticut, 1963. *Dissertation Abstracts,* XXIV (1964), 4679-4680.

"Taylor's poetry must be seen in its private instead of its public character before final critical judgment is made about his reputation as a poet." This private quality of Taylor's verse, and not his lack of orthodoxy, is what caused him not to publish. Hence it is not fair to compare the communicative success of Taylor's poetry with the English devotional poets.

298 Nicolaisen, Peter. "Die Bildlichkeit in Edward Taylors *Preparatory Meditations*." Unpublished doctoral dissertation, Kiel, 1964. (See Nicolaisen, No. 99.)

299 Peterson, Richard. "The 'Art of Meditation' in Edward Taylor's *Preparatory Meditations*." Unpublished dissertation, Kent State University, 1967.

300 Russell, Gene. "Dialectal and Phonetic Features of Edward Taylor's Rhymes: A Brief Study Based Upon a Computer Concordance of His Poems." Unpublished doctoral dissertation, University of Wisconsin, 1970.

301 Scheick, William Joseph. "The Will and the Word: The Experience of Conversion in the Poetry of Edward Taylor." Unpublished doctoral dissertation, University of Illinois, 1969. *Dissertation Abstracts International*, XXX (1970), 2979A.

The theme of Taylor's verse is that "the search for conversion was, in Taylor's terms, a quest for love." Discusses the importance of the will as the focus of the *Meditations*.

302 Shepherd, Emma Louise. "The Metaphysical Conceit in the Poetry of Edward Taylor." Unpublished doctoral dissertation, University of North Carolina, 1960. *Dissertation Abstracts*, XXI (1961), 1942.

Defines "metaphysical conceit" as its meaning has developed from the seventeenth century to the present. Discusses the "predominance of the conceit" in Taylor's metaphorical technique, both in the *Meditations* and in *Gods Determinations*, showing that he is to that extent a metaphysical poet. Feels that his best poems are the one-third or so which develop one "basic conceit" throughout most of the poem.

303 Smith, Roy Harold. "A Study of the Platonic Heritage of Love in the Poetry of Edward Taylor." Unpublished doctoral dissertation, Bowling Green State University, 1969. *Dissertation Abstracts International*, XXX (1970), 4466A.

Platonism provides "an expanded cultural framework for explaining Taylor's 'unusualness' as a Puritan." Through a comparison of ideas from Platonic dialogues, *The Courtier* and the *Enneads*, demonstrates that the idea of the enhanced soul and the intellectual vision of love are central to Taylor's devotional poetry.

304 Stanford, Donald E. "An Edition of the Complete Poetical Works of Edward Taylor." Unpublished doctoral dissertation, Stanford University, 1953. *Dissertation Abstracts*, XIV (1954), 528.

The basis for Stanford's edition of *The Poems* (No. 3). Includes the most complete and reliable biography of Taylor, a shorter version of which is published in Stanford's Introduction to *The Poems.*

305 Wack, Thomas George. "The Imagery of Edward Taylor's *Preparatory Meditations*." Unpublished doctoral dissertation, University of Notre Dame, 1961. *Dissertation Abstracts*, XXII (1962), 2389.

Reaffirms Taylor's Calvinism in spite of the influence of the "Counter-Reformation habits of spirituality," especially in his metaphysical style and baroque images. Taylor's "skillful use of extremely domestic imagery and colloquial language makes his devotional poems outstanding among those of the English metaphysicals."

306 Wiley, Elizabeth. "Sources of Imagery in the Poetry of Edward Taylor." Unpublished doctoral dissertation, University of Pittsburgh, 1962. *Dissertation Abstracts*, XXIII (1962), 2122-2123.

On the basis of the books in Taylor's library, which Sewall is reported to have lent him, and the 1611 Authorized Version of the Bible, concludes that Taylor's sources of imagery "tied his works to the mainstream of poetry written by his contemporaries, who were also influenced by the same body of literature."

Index of Authors